SECURE
by DESIGN

A leader's guide
to keeping
cybercriminals
out of your
business

René-Sylvain Bédard

Re think

First published in Great Britain in 2025
by Rethink Press (www.rethinkpress.com)

© Copyright René-Sylvain Bédard

Cover image licensed by Ingram Image

*To my mother, Rollande, the untameable spirit.
Who showed me the way of entrepreneurship
and how to never give up, to be curious, how to
figure out things and make things happen.*

*To my children, who altered my life path, and
to my wife, Marie-Hélène, who anchored me
in the truth and brought all this together.*

Providing the space to make all this possible.

Contents

Foreword   1

Introduction   7

1   Who Needs Cybersecurity?   15

The myths that can end your company   18

The SECURE way   25

Summary   35

2   Survey   37

Know thyself   38

Know your enemy   63

Know your score   68

Summary   69

3 Educate   **71**

Educate yourself   72

Engage your executive team   107

Empower your staff   111

Summary   112

4 Construct   **115**

Before you start   115

Draw a plan   116

Get ready to receive logs: Create an
alarm central   118

Strengthen your identity   121

Build your security system   127

Enable auditing   136

Set up a monitoring service   138

Keep registries, logs and controls   139

Problem solving   140

Summary   142

5 Unify   **145**

People   147

Technology   152

Processes   159

Ecosystem   163

Summary   166

6 Review   **169**

Constant awareness   170

Managing alerts   172

Automated response   173

Outsourcing   174

Annual audit   176

Carry out simulations   177

Intrusion testing   178

Fixing what is found   183

Prepare for the worst   186

Summary   195

7 Evolve   **197**

New processes, evolving processes   198

New people   198

New technologies   199

New partners in the ecosystem   199

Most importantly: new threats   200

Using AI to your advantage   204

The next leap: Quantum technology   211

Summary   213

Conclusion   **215**

Notes   **219**

Resources   225

Acknowledgments   227

The Author   229

Foreword

As a business owner and COO of a global organization, I spend a lot of time on planes. Like
me, you probably know the routine well. You arrive at
the airport and quickly get absorbed into a sea of other
travelers, all trying to get to where they're going. You
move through airline check-in, security, customs and
airport shops in unison with this newfound group
of kindred spirits, before eventually arriving at your
departure gate. Hours of preparation, getting out the
door and organized chaos at the airport has finally
brought you here... and this is all before you board
the plane!

Eventually, you sit down in your assigned seat and
take a breath. It dawns on you what a miracle of
human ingenuity and modern flight technology is.

Unless you're an engineer at Boeing or work in the airline industry, it's hard to comprehend the level of systems and infrastructure required to allow this giant hollow capsule to hurl hundreds of human beings through the atmosphere at 600 miles per hour, before landing safely back on Earth. It does all this with an unparalleled track record of safety and efficacy we often take for granted.

Now Imagine your business as that modern airliner, soaring through the skies, carrying thousands of passengers – your data, your assets, your reputation – every day. Just like an airline, your organization's success hinges on the seamless operation of complex systems, constant vigilance and a commitment to safety. Cybersecurity is the sophisticated control panel of your aircraft, a critical instrument providing real-time alerts and guidance. Just as pilots rely on ground control for vital information and support, your cybersecurity defenses must work in harmony with every layer of your organization.

As a CEO, who may also be a frequent flyer, you'll notice that the parallels between aviation and cybersecurity are striking. Pilots and ground control teams must anticipate and mitigate risks, maintain strict protocols and ensure that every component of the aircraft functions flawlessly. In the same way, your cybersecurity strategy must be proactive, comprehensive and integrated into the fabric of your business.

I work with CEOs and entrepreneurs every day, and I can say with confidence that most don't look at their business in this way. The safety and security of their data, assets and critical information is often an after-thought. And why wouldn't it be? I mean, how likely is it really that a breach will affect them?

In *Secure by Design*, René-Sylvain Bédard makes it clear that most businesses, big and small, are woefully underprepared and ill-equipped to deal with security breaches in today's world of sophisticated cybercrime. If you suspect that this is you too, then frankly, it's not your fault. Considering the complicated ecosystem of various technologies – Firewalls, DMZ, SIEM, EDR, identity and access management, and many more – it's not hard to see how protecting against the pos-sibility of something going wrong quickly becomes a 'future priority' and gets kicked down the road until a seismic event ripples through the company… when it's too late to stop it.

However, these events are no longer 'long-tail' pos-sibilities. They're far more frequent and more serious than most CEOs realize, and these CEOs are often the most terrified and technically ill-equipped to know how to protect their organization against these threats.

This book will introduce you to the SECURE method, a simple and easy-to-understand model and a holis-tic approach to fortifying your business against cyber threats. This method isn't just about deploying the latest technology; it's about creating a culture of security that permeates every aspect of your organization.

Imagine your cybersecurity much like the foundational architecture of a skyscraper: architects, builders and tradespeople collaborate to construct a towering structure that can withstand the elements and the test of time. Similarly, you will learn that your cybersecurity framework must be meticulously planned, expertly executed and continuously maintained to protect your digital assets from ever-evolving threats.

Think of the SECURE method as your blueprint for constructing that resilient cybersecurity skyscraper:

- **Survey:** Just as architects survey the land and environment before designing a building, you must understand your business landscape and identify vulnerabilities.

- **Educate:** Builders and tradespeople must be skilled and knowledgeable to execute the architect's vision. Similarly, your team must be trained to recognize and respond to cyber threats.

- **Construct:** The construction phase involves laying a strong foundation and building robust structures. In cybersecurity, this means implementing a multi-layered defense strategy.

- **Unify:** A skyscraper's stability depends on the seamless integration of its various components.

Your cybersecurity protocols must harmonize people, processes and technology.

- **Review:** Like engineers regularly inspect buildings for safety, you must continuously test and refine your defenses.

- **Evolve:** Buildings are upgraded to meet new safety standards. Your cybersecurity measures must also adapt to new threats and incorporate the latest technologies.

Take the example of a small business owner, John, which René-Sylvain recounts in the chapters that follow. John believed his company, which underwrites patents, was too insignificant to attract cybercriminals. One Friday, his company was attacked. His systems were restored over the weekend, but by Wednesday, John learned that his entire patent database was being sold on the dark web. The fallout was devastating: legal battles, financial loss and a shattered reputation. This scenario is not uncommon and serves as a stark reminder that no business is too small to be targeted.

The SECURE method will guide you through the intricacies of safeguarding your business. It's about transforming your cybersecurity approach from a reactive stance to a proactive, strategic one. By integrating these principles, you will not only protect your business but enhance its resilience and competitive edge.

Like business growth, cybersecurity is a journey – not a destination. It requires continuous vigilance, investment and commitment from the top down. As leaders, it's our duty to safeguard our organizations against the unseen threats that lurk in the dark shadows of the web (or even within our organizations). This book is your map to navigating this perilous (and often mysterious) landscape, turning potential vulnerabilities into fortified strengths.

I hope you can embrace the principles outlined in *Secure by Design* and let this be your wake-up call. You are not just protecting data; you are ensuring the continuity, integrity and prosperity of your business.

We all have our part to play to make the internet a safe place for businesses like ours to operate. You owe it to your customers, your staff, stakeholders and investors to protect their livelihood, their reputation and their investments. There's too much at stake not to do so.

This book will show you the way.

Mike Reid
Co-founder, Dent Global
https://dent.global

Introduction

As the owner of a small or medium business, you may think that you are too small to be attacked by cybercriminals, that you have nothing worth stealing anyway, that all your data is in the cloud, so it must be safe, and that you have insurance that will cover you in the unlikely event of an attack, so there is nothing for you to worry about.

Think again.

These days, there is nothing small about small and medium businesses. It is estimated that 52.3% of Canada's economy is owed to SMEs, according to Innovation, Science and Economic Development Canada.[1] Here is how this is reflected worldwide:

- Worldwide, it is estimated that SMEs represent about 90% of businesses and over 70% of employment.

- They contribute over 50% of gross domestic product (GDP) in emerging economies and up to 70% of the global world product.

- As an example, in the Canadian private sector, SMEs provide a recorded 79.5% of all employment.[2]

At the same time, the vast majority of cyberattacks are against SMEs. According to a report from Asterès, a leading French research agency, 86.7% of all reported attacks in France in 2022 were against that category of business.[3]

Even if you know all this and are conscious that you are the perfect prey for a cybercriminal, you may not be fully aware of just how insidious and pernicious such attacks can be, let alone how best to protect yourself against them.

I was recently contacted by the owner of a small business that underwrites patents. John (not his real name) had spent twenty years building his company from nothing. Then, one Friday morning, he suffered a cyberattack. John had all his systems managed by a service provider who assured him that they would be up and running again by Monday morning. Sure enough, after a weekend of agonizing worry, John found everything back to normal and could resume work as if nothing had happened.

Or could he?

On Wednesday morning, John received a call from the provincial authorities advising him that his entire patent database – a list of all patents (and their owners) who were served by his company – was for sale on the dark web. At this point his problem was no longer a technological challenge, but a legal minefield – one that took John twelve months to clear at a cost of over 200,000 dollars. Hard-earned clear profit, just gone.

A cyberattack creates a tsunami of often unforeseen consequences. Your employees will ask you whether they will be paid that month, whether their jobs are secure, and even whether the company will still exist in the morning. Your providers and subcontractors will suffer financially and, if their systems are linked to yours, possibly also experience similar attacks. Your customers will question whether to continue to do business with you or to turn to your competitors instead. If their data – even perhaps their personal identity – has been stolen, how will you be able to apologize, let alone compensate them, adequately?

The effects can be nothing less than catastrophic.

It is all over the internet: 'Sixty per cent of all attacked companies don't survive for more than a year.'[4] This quote, from *INC.* magazine, was never real, but it fires the imagination.[5] One can easily understand why. Consider for a minute a small business that overnight gets hit with a bill for many hundreds of thousands of dollars. How many are ready to face such an extinction event? Some would close immediately after the attack, while others would fall within a few months from the financial and reputational impact. Of the rest, few would make it out alive.

A cyberattack won't only ruin your business. It will also have human consequences – many of them undiscussed, but no less real for that. To begin with, you are likely to be blamed for allowing the attack to happen, and you will feel guilty and incompetent. You (and your IT staff) will need to work around the clock to (try to) recover systems and data, putting you all under additional pressure and stress, with a direct impact on your family lives. Burnout rates resulting from such pressure are going through the roof. According to ISACA, 51% of cybersecurity professionals have had a prescription to manage stress and 21% (over one in five) are considering leaving the field due to stressful conditions.[6] Over a quarter (28%) of Chief Information Security Officers (CISO) are leaving their jobs due to burnout.

Over the years, my company has had to recover numerous small businesses from cybersecurity incidents – ransomware attacks, to be precise. It is a heart-wrenching experience to see a small business owner, who has poured their heart and soul into creating a successful business only to have it wiped out within a few hours, and then to be bullied into giving away their life savings to some unseen criminals...

If you want none of this to happen to you, *Secure by Design* will show you how to defend yourself.

I was trained by some of the leading experts in cybersecurity and have almost thirty years of technology experience. I spent my nights in the 90s learning HTML and became a lead Microsoft architect before setting up my own consulting agency, Indominus, in 2017. I have been blessed with a wide range of experience, with a client list that includes governments, banks, telecoms providers and aerospace manufacturers, as well as SMEs. Indominus is committed to combating cybercrime worldwide, using cutting-edge technologies and innovative approaches to protect both organizations and individuals.

I call cybercrime 'bullying' because entrepreneurs recovering from ransomware attacks are like kids in high schools who have been bullied into giving up their lunch money. I have seen it so many times. This is why I chose to become a cyber-defender – to protect 'defenceless' businesses. I could not simply stand there and do nothing.

As part of this commitment, Indominus has created the SECURE method to enable you, the small business owner, to become aware of what is happening in your environment, of what is crucial for your business to keep operating under an attack, and of what you need to do to prevent it from being attacked in the first place.

The SECURE method consists of the following steps:

- Survey

- Educate

- Construct

- Unify

- Review

- Evolve

We start by *Surveying* your business – deconstructing it into different systems and processes, so that you can better understand where your cybersecurity weaknesses are. I go on to explain how to cultivate cybersecurity awareness within your company by *Educating* both yourself and your staff. You will then be able to *Construct* a customized security strategy for your business.

Cybersecurity isn't just about technology; it is also about processes and people. You must therefore *Unify* your new security protocols across your whole business, as well as throughout your 'ecosystem' of suppliers and subcontractors. Since cybersecurity is a constantly changing challenge, you will need to regularly *Review* and test the security measures you have put in place and ensure that they continually *Evolve* to meet new threats.

In these chapters, you will learn about naming conventions and zero-trust strategies, about foundational services and enclaves, about the growing impact of AI, about ChatGPT and Microsoft Copilot, and you will learn how some of these tools can actually support you against cybercriminals. Most importantly, you will discover how to identify the things you most need to protect, and you will understand your critical systems and have confidence that the proper monitoring and warning procedures are in place to mitigate the effects of a cyberattack. Critically, you will also know how your opponent thinks, where they are most likely to attack you, and how.

To use a simple analogy, your company might not currently even have battery-operated smoke detectors in some of your offices and you would not know if a fire started. You and your staff might make it out alive, but the building and all its contents – in other words, your entire business – would most likely be ashes by the morning.

After reading *Secure by Design,* your house will be in order. You will have a proper fence around your lot, an alarm system linked to a central hub, and, more importantly, your most critical data will be in a safe place, under multiple layers of security, not exposed with the rest of your data. If smoke is detected or a window broken, you will be aware, have time to react, and you will be able to save your house.

Do you see the difference?

Let us not kid ourselves: protecting your business from cyberattacks will not be easy and no system will ever be 100% hacker-proof. At the end of the day, your goal is to secure your company's future as best you can. Without adequate cybersecurity, it may not have one. With the SECURE system in place, it stands a much better chance of surviving.

ONE

Who Needs Cybersecurity?

L ike me, you are probably old enough to remember life BC – before computers – or at least before the internet. How simple, almost idyllic, it seems now. Even multinational corporations used to run effectively and efficiently without a screen or a mouse or a keyboard in sight – other than a typewriter keyboard, of course. No data storage issues, no input errors, no backup problems, no memory losses or system failures, let alone cyberattacks.

Today – barely forty years since computers started appearing in workplaces – we can scarcely imagine life without them. In little more than a generation, all business processes have been completely altered, and a whole array of risks and threats and dangers have appeared that we could hardly even have dreamed of back then.

Consider running a hotel with 200 rooms, where, thanks to modern technology, you can know at the click of a mouse not only how much each and every guest has paid for their room, but also what food and drink they have ordered, what films they have watched, what they have consumed from their mini bar, even whether they had a shirt laundered or ironed.

Now imagine what would happen if the hotel's computers unexpectedly went down and all that information was lost. Consider the impact. You would suddenly know nothing about any of your 200 guests. You wouldn't know how much to charge them. You wouldn't even be *able* to charge them – or pay your staff. If it took you a month to restore normal operations, the cost would be astronomical.

Let's work it out:

- 100 employees, at an average of $20 per hour = $480,000 in unpaid salaries.

- 200 rooms, at an average of $200 per night = $1,200,000 in lost revenue.

- Thirty days of around-the-clock technical services = $300,000.

- Legal fees and crisis management = $200,000.

- New computer systems required (hardware, software, etc) = $100,000.

We are at over $2 million already, without counting what you would owe to goods and services providers, not to mention the value of the potential data loss and damage to your reputation.

It would be enough to make you go back to accounting with pen and paper.

All this, and worse, can be caused by a cyberattack, and yet most small business owners are ill-equipped – or not equipped at all – either to defend themselves against attack or to deal with the consequences of an attack, should it happen.

Recent reports indicate that:

- 47% of businesses with fewer than fifty employees have no cybersecurity budget

- 51% of small businesses have no cybersecurity measures in place at all

- 36% of small businesses are 'not at all concerned' about cyberattacks

- Only 17% of small businesses encrypt data

- One-third of businesses with fifty or fewer employees rely on free, consumer-grade cybersecurity solutions

- 59% of small business owners with no cybersecurity measures in place believe that their business is too small to be attacked[7]

The myths that can end your company

The last of these statistics points to one of the five myths that comfort small and medium business owners at night – the myths that cybercrime only happens to other people, that they are too small to be attacked, that they host nothing of value, that their data is safe in the cloud, and that, in the unlikely event that anything terrible does happen, their insurance will cover them.

Let us debunk those myths right now.

Cybercrime only happens to others

It is a trait of most humans, to think that bad things will only happen to others. That can't happen to you. But at some point, it hits you. You become the unlucky other. Since 2021, cyberattacks have risen over 300% according to the latest *Microsoft Digital Defense Report* – a threefold rise.[8] None of the companies that were hit by ransomware over the last decade thought they were chosen or deserved to be attacked. None. This is no different to saying that a car accident will never happen to you. That can only be true if you are not going out of your house. Even as a pedestrian, it can happen to you. If you have a business and you are using some kind of technology and, God forbid, if you are making money, then yes, you are a potential target.

Following an encounter I once had with a dairy farmer, I came up with a question that I now often ask in my presentations: do you believe that a cow requires cybersecurity? The crowd usually answers that of course they don't.

I then explain to them that the latest development in AgTech (agricultural technologies) means that a team of two farmers can milk 1,000 cows. This amazing advancement allows us to break the physical limitations that used to plague farms. All these devices are connected to the internet in order for sensor data to be collected. I asked one of its makers if they secured the connections. He answered there was no need as it was only sensor data, not interesting to any cybercriminals.

There was the door – the way in for a cybercriminal who will do anything to get to their goal, which is bullying you into giving them your money.

Hence, a bad actor, thousands of kilometres away, can stop all the farm's robots cold. Stop the cows from being milked and send a nice email for a ransom. With no milk, the dairy farm would be out of revenue for months and would probably collapse. What if this attack is executed on 100 farms? They could all be stopped at once. We are talking about millions in lost revenues, all because cows don't require cybersecurity, and the magic thinking that these things only happen to others.

We're too small to be attacked

The root of this myth is the assumption that cybercriminals are like fishermen: that they carefully choose their spots and then cast a line into the water to catch a particular fish. Nothing can be further from the truth.

Cybercriminals today operate in networks, constantly offering services to new members to make them more efficient and sharing their profits throughout the network. They are no longer individuals in hoodies in basements; this is the age of dark corporations with objectives and quotas, of 'ransomware as a service'. Not lone fishermen, but fleets of trawlers capturing all they can, by the ton.

When they send out a phishing email with the aim of infiltrating a company, months before the actual attack, they do not send ten or twenty; they send between 100,000 and 500,000.

What does that say about small and medium businesses? It says that you make up the greatest volume of fish – you are the largest group in the sea. For each large corporation, there are thousands of small and medium businesses. As an example, according to the renowned data site Statista, there were, in 2021, 8,365 companies with over 1,000 employees, compared to the total of 16,435,439 companies below that number.[9] According to those numbers, enterprises constitute 0.051% of all companies, so they may get targeted as the bigger fish, but never as often as the largest shoal in the sea.

We have nothing worth stealing

If you are in business, it is unlikely that you have nothing to steal. Apart from artists and artisans, who are paid in cash for services that only their talented hands can provide, pretty much all businesses today have valuable customer and employee information. More importantly, if you are in business, you must be making money; hence, you have the one thing that cybercriminals crave above all else: money.

After a short time, they will know how much money you have. They will spend months in your systems, sniffing around for clues – in documents, emails, financial statements, human resources files or customer databases – until they have figured out two things: what is important to you and how much you are willing (and able) to pay to get it back. Yes, this can (and most likely will) include deleting or infecting your backups to solidify their claim.

Then they will send you a ransom demand. (Whether you decide to pay or not is up to you, but you should understand that as long as victims will pay ransoms – and the attackers make money – cyberattacks will continue.)

Our data is safe in the cloud

Don't kid yourself. This is not how the cloud works. Although Microsoft (and most other cloud providers) are secure environments, they also have what is known as a Shared Responsibility Matrix. This means that for your data, your research and your business intelligence, to be isolated and to remain fully yours, Microsoft will not access it. They will not subject it to their own security procedures, which might alter the structure of your data and potentially disrupt your business. That would go against the reasons for offering you space in the cloud. Instead, they guarantee that the foundational, underlying systems will be secured and defended.

What do I mean by the underlying system? Picture that you are hiring a security company. They will guard the access to your lot, make sure that no one is messing with access to your house, and that you have electricity and communications, but they will not manage what happens inside your house. Same here: you are a tenant within the cloud provider's infrastructure. He will make sure the gate to your space is guarded and that you have everything you need, but what happens within your company, on services and servers that he is leasing you, is completely your responsibility.

Here is the matrix, based on information from the Microsoft website.[10]

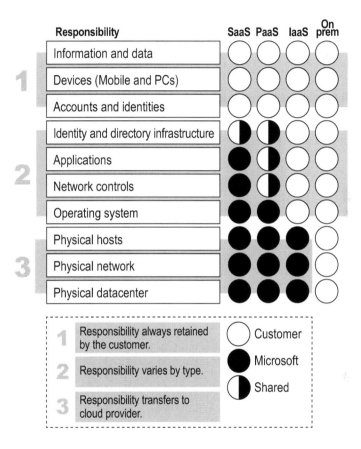

Here is a little refresher for those of you who did not attend the class on cloud acronyms and abbreviations:

- **On-Prem:** This means on-premises – ie your servers and services are running on equipment that you own and manage and for which you are wholly responsible.

- **IaaS:** Infrastructure-as-a-Service. This means that you are running your services on someone else's hardware and infrastructure components. A good example here is migrating your own database server to the cloud.

- **PaaS:** With Platform-as-a-Service, you are asking the cloud service provider to also manage the underlying operating system, to keep it up to date and ensure that it runs smoothly. In this example, you are deploying a new database server in the cloud, with the service provider's optimized and managed version of the software.

- **SaaS:** With Software-as-a-Service, you are the consumer. You do not care how it works, as long as it works. You are consuming the service. Note that, even if you are far away from managing every aspect of your database service on-premise, you are still responsible for your users, your data and the devices that access the said service.

Note that your devices' security is your responsibility, as are your staff's passwords, and if any of your team chooses to share a confidential document with someone outside the business, no amount of cloud security will help you.

We have adequate insurance

Let us go back to the fire analogy I gave you earlier. What would buildings and contents insurance provide you if there was a fire in your offices? It would allow you to rebuild, buy back furniture and equipment and return to a normal life in perhaps four to six months. In other words, your insurance company will send you a cheque once your premises are in ashes (if you are lucky).

Far better – and usually much cheaper – to avoid a fire than to recover from one.

Don't misunderstand me, insurance is necessary, but it cannot be the only component of your business protection plan. You also need proactive services that will enable you to react to a 'fire' *before* it reduces everything to ashes. As I said before, having a few battery-powered smoke detectors is far from adequate.

With proper cybersecurity, you might lose a device or a server, but you will survive the attack and still have a company to run. Instead of playing phoenix, you will live to fight another day.

In the remaining chapters of this book, I will describe my SECURE method of protecting your business from cyberattacks. Here is an overview of the steps in the method.

The SECURE way

SECURE is a six-step method that enables any business owner to go from total unawareness of the dangers in their environment and complete lack of visibility of their vulnerabilities, to having a complete understanding of their cybersecurity 'score', an in-depth knowledge of what is required to improve it, and a confident command of the tools available to defend their business.

S for Survey

The fundamental concept of this method is that you cannot protect yourself against unknown dangers. Just as you cannot improve anything if you don't measure its performance, you cannot build adequate defences unless you know what you are defending yourself against. It is essential to understand what are likely targets for cybercriminals, and what are not.

I once worked with a large health organization that wanted to implement a new backup system. When I asked them to categorize their various classes of systems and data in terms of criticality and priority, there was an uneasy silence. They didn't know what these were, let alone which ones were more or less important.

That is when I explained to them, 'You cannot simply back up everything and consider that the receptionist's Spotify playlist has the same value as a patient's x-rays.' The general belief is that, if you back up everything, you are safe. At some point, however, a 'blanket' backup becomes a hindrance.

If you have a vast amount of data to restore and you do not know in what sequence it needs to be restored, a few things will happen:

- When testing your backup, you might use frivolous data while your critical files might be corrupted. You will only find this out when you need to restore them. At that point, it is too late.

- The effort and time required to restore everything is unnecessary and a waste of resources.

- In the event of an incident or a crisis, you will not know where to start.

- Where an incremental backup might get essential services back online in a few hours, a complete restoration will take weeks.

- You will not be able to apply the best security to protect your most sensitive data. High-level encryption requires lots of processing and has an impact on backup speed, so it should be used only on highly confidential and sensitive data. If you want to back up everything, that level of security has to be sacrificed.

So, in this first step of the SECURE method (Chapter 2), I will show you how to map your critical data and the systems they run on, which will help you save precious resources and prioritize (and accelerate) recovery.

E for Educate

In the second step in the method, you will realize that you cannot secure your business by yourself. Just as it takes a village to educate a child, you will need all the members of your community to make your business secure.

That means that everyone in your company needs to be trained in cybersecurity, their awareness levels need to be raised and they must be made accountable for their actions. It also means that security will need to be integrated into processes and technology and regularly reviewed.

Cybersecurity training cannot be optional. Humans have always been the weakest link in any security system, but now that we have tools that can generate human-like emails, voicemails and videos, users must have sharper reflexes than ever.

Here is a glimpse of the types of activity that your training will need to include:

- **Management onboarding tools:** As the owner, you will not be able to alter corporate culture without your lieutenants. You need them to row with you.

- **Awareness campaigns:** The first step to strengthening your security is making sure your staff are aware of all the possible dangers. They may make mistakes and stumble, but if they can't recognize a threat, they will not inform you of it, and you will never know.

- **Sample policies and agreements:** As it will also be important to make your user's community accountable for their actions, make it real for them. You will need to define what is acceptable within your walls, and what the end user will be responsible for.

- **Measurable objectives:** Since you can't improve what you don't measure, training will give you some interesting metrics that you can follow to demonstrate progress.

- **Spear phishing:** Launch a phishing attack against your staff and see who gets caught. Those employees are then given targeted training so that they understand the risks and take adequate precautions.

- **Fire drill:** Just like a normal fire drill, everything is shut down for a period and you then check your recovery is successful. That plan will need to be refined if drills fail – as the first few almost certainly will do.

Like any training programme, cybersecurity training will require education, since fear and resistance to change will be your biggest challenge, as in any new project. We will explore the most common reasons for resistance and fear in Chapter 3.

C for Construct

This is the part of the SECURE method where you start building your defences. Now that you know what must be protected and everyone understands the importance of that protection, you will start building defensive layers, like those in a medieval fort, to make sure that it remains safe.

The end goal of this phase is simple: to make stealing your data more costly in effort than the potential financial reward for doing so.

I will show you how to create the rules, the assets and the improvements to your processes to ensure that your data is properly structured and protected in line with its criticality level, and that the systems on which this data depends are also reliable and secured.

Part of this discussion will focus on implementing or choosing the right technology to support your defensive programme.

U for Unify

You are never as strong as when you work together. In this part of the method, you will harmonize people, processes and technology to close any gaps you found in your initial survey, to make sure that your staff are properly educated and that the systems you have constructed are operating effectively. Just as you tested your backups to ensure that you could restore your data, so now you will test your entire recovery process to be sure that you will survive an attack.

To continue our medieval fort analogy, you will test your barricades by simulating attacks both from within your company and from outside to make sure that your defences hold. When the enemy comes knocking, they won't hold anything back. They will throw everything they have at you to gain access to your data and your money. You need to be sure that your company will still be standing in the morning.

R for Review

So how did it go? Are you still standing? It is essential to review what just happened. Did your plan work? Were you really ready? How vulnerable are you still? Remember: this was only a simulation. Any weaknesses in the plan that have been revealed must now be addressed so that you are properly protected if a real incident occurs.

Let me give you an example.

We were once doing a security audit for a health region authority. One of my team members oversaw what we call 'intrusion (or penetration) testing'.

We were sitting at the conference table for the project kick-off, and he asked to go to the washroom.

The manager accompanied him, and she came back without him. At this point, I knew: they were compromised.

When he came back from the washroom, he looked at me and I could see the hint of a smile on his face. Mischief accomplished.

Six weeks later, he was sitting in his home office, 300 kilometres from the customer. During a conference call, he told the CISO (Chief Information Security Officer) to look on his desktop for a text file with his first name.

There it was. The file was there, in clear text. He had full access to his desktop.

Five minutes distraction. A few weeks of shadow work.

Environment compromised.

What must be taken away from this anecdote is that you can have training, technology and processes, but there is still a need to be a deep review and auditing process in place to catch potential human errors.

It is not enough to implement solutions; you must be sure that the process, the people and the technology are all working together.

E for Evolve

As you will by now be aware, cybersecurity can never be static. The threats to your security are evolving daily, especially with the ongoing AI revolution. Your security systems must also evolve if you are to keep pace with the cybercriminal gangs. Again, you might not be able to do this alone and will need partners to support you.

In this phase of the SECURE method, we will be making what author, coach and business strategist Tony Robbins calls CANI – constant and never-ending improvements.[11] Your systems and methods need to become more and more resilient, and your people ever-more critical when it comes to data authenticity and veracity.

A government agency in Canada recently had a 'water incident' during which its server farm, which was located in the basement, was flooded. The good news was that the agency had a recovery plan, which had been thoroughly tested over the years since its creation in the late 90s. A few weeks into the recovery process, however, management started wondering when email was planned to come back online. Only then did they realize that email was never added to the high-priority items because it was a secondary system back in the 90s and the plan had not been updated.

Through awareness, you will get reactivity, which will allow you to stop bad actors in their tracks. No matter where they come from.

Key points when it comes to the evolution of your cybersecurity strategy include:

- **Staying awake:** Cybercrime never sleeps, so your data and systems must be secure even when everyone is at home resting or away on holiday. Is there always someone on the lookout in case of an attack outside of office hours?

- **Being ever curious:** If you notice any strange behaviours within your environment, do you question them?

- **Looking within:** Threats can also come from inside your organization, and the fact that they do does not make them any less dangerous. Are you looking inwards as well as outwards?

- **Keeping up to date:** New technology can support you in your cybersecurity journey and help you keep up with the cybercriminals, or they can pose new threats to your safety. AI is a great example; are you going to use it to further secure your data and systems, or ignore it as just another fad?

We will look at these in more detail, as well as at other ways to keep your cybersecurity evolving, in Chapter 7.

Summary

Your company runs on data, which has to be protected. If it's not, you risk losing everything. Your company's survival cannot be based on myths. In this chapter we have seen that:

- Cyberattacks do not only happen to others; when it comes to cybersecurity, everyone is a target

- No one is 'too small' to be attacked; if you have customers or money, you are a potential victim and it is not a matter of if but when

- Your data is not 'safe in the cloud'; you are still responsible for its security

- Having insurance is essential, but it cannot be the only part of your cybersecurity strategy

You need a comprehensive cybersecurity strategy, which is enshrined in the SECURE method described in this book. It will show you how to:

- **Survey** your environment, your data, your processes and your systems to allow you to know them intimately, allowing you to create an appropriate defence strategy

- **Educate** your teams to become aware of the risks and threats that exist within your environment, which will enable you to create the conditions to make them accountable and share responsibility for your information security

- **Construct** the processes and technology to repair any weaknesses exposed by your initial survey

- **Unify** all the building blocks of your strategy – people, processes and technologies – and then test that new barricade to see if it holds

- **Review** your strategy and make sure that you are ready when a real attack occurs

- **Evolve** at the same speed as the increasingly sophisticated methods used by cybercriminals

TWO

Survey

Before you can start building defences, you must survey both the landscape your company operates within and the modus operandi of its potential enemies: cybercriminals.

First, you must examine your business and categorize not only what needs to be protected but also what it depends on to function – your foundational services. You may need a specific software or service to run your company, but if you no longer have a computer, you are still unable to work. If you are an engineering firm and you recover all your plans, that is great, but until you have access to your network and AutoCAD, they are just files, and you still can't work.

Know thyself

This first step involves evaluating the current data landscape, making a comprehensive assessment of existing security measures, identifying potential vulnerabilities, understanding the data flows within your organization, and determining areas of potential risk.

I will look at each of these areas in detail before explaining who cybercriminals are and how they operate.

Viewing the landscape

We can compare your data landscape to a piece of land that requires a topographical survey. You need to find out what is out there, and what it is used for. You don't need to identify every blade of grass or every leaf in that land, but you do need to know where the rivers are and where the peaks and valleys are so that you can create a safe journey through it.

It is important to understand that you cannot do this alone. Data means different things to different people within your organization, and each will assign different priorities and criticalities to different types of data. Your first step is to identify exactly what your company's data consists of.

Think of your data as chess pieces: your most critical data as the king. If you lose your king, the game is over, so you must make sure it is safe and that it has a place to retreat to that is well-defended against the advancing enemy.

Not all data is contained in Word documents and Excel files. Here are a few examples of the types of data your company almost certainly holds – the loss of which could really hurt:

- Accounting database
- Customer Relationship Management database (CRM) containing your customers' data
- Your human resources data, including your employees' personal information
- Mailing lists
- Domain name system (DNS), access to which would allow criminals to redirect any of your web locations to their own
- Digital assets relating to your brand
- Your website
- Your social network accounts
- Digitally signed contracts and legal documents, some of which may be hosted at a third party's location
- Compromising videos, SMS, emails or other chats
- Web browsing history

You might not consider the last two items on this list 'data' that needs protecting, but when it comes to security, they can cause you the most concern. I was once presenting to a room full of executives, telling them all about the need for cybersecurity. I could see them nodding dutifully – even, in some cases, nodding off – until I said that, if their laptops were infiltrated, the last six months of their browsing history would be visible, and they suddenly became really nervous. One means of extorsion exercised by cybercriminals is a threat to expose all those who have used your corporate devices to access pornographic and illicit sites. Sometimes, such history logs can expose the merger or research that the management team has been doing, which can also create market confusion.

You must therefore consider all possible data types and create a grid that will make sense specifically for your company.

	Restricted	Confidential	Internal	Public
Administration	Business strategies, M&A	Growth plan, Revenues	Processes, Methods	Branding, Culture
Human resources	Salaries, Employee files	Resumes, Recruiting methodologies	Policies, Procedures, etc.	Job posting
Sales	Pricing information	Marketing strategies	Service offers, Statement of work	Product marketing

As you can see from the diagram above, your grid consists of several 'buckets' of data, such as:

- **Public or informational data:** The type that is readily available online, which does not need protecting

- **Confidential data:** Including customers' or employees' personal information

- **Internal data:** Your trade secrets, data that belongs to your company and that would hurt its future if exposed

- **Restricted data:** Data that is not for everyone but only for managers or directors, such as financial data or data on salaries

The idea is not to create 100 buckets, or the model will become so complicated that no one will use it. What you want are essentially sensitivity labels that will help you to categorize and protect the various types of data according to their criticality.

How you do this is up to you, but keeping it simple is often best. One of the best classification models is the 'traffic light' system: green for data that can readily be shared, yellow for data that can be shared only with certain parties, and red for data that you do not share or disclose to anyone.

Once you have this system in place, every time you create new data, it should be classified so that the appropriate rules and security procedures automatically apply to it. That is the easy part. The hard bit is classifying your existing data, which, depending on how long you have been in business, there could be an awful lot of.

There are two pieces of good news. First, tools exist that will help you identify and classify your data. Second, there is most likely already a system in place within your company that, for example, makes accounting data available only to your finance staff and human resources data available only to that department. All you need to do is turn those physical or logical restrictions into security barriers. I will show you how to do this in Chapter 4.

Laying the foundations

Now that you are aware of what your data is and where it is, you must figure out what services and software it relies on to be used.

Data all by itself is mostly useless. Most of the time, it has dependencies – requirements for it to be usable. Just as a document might require Word to be usable, or an architect's plan may need AutoCAD to be read or modified, other types of data depend on particular software or systems.

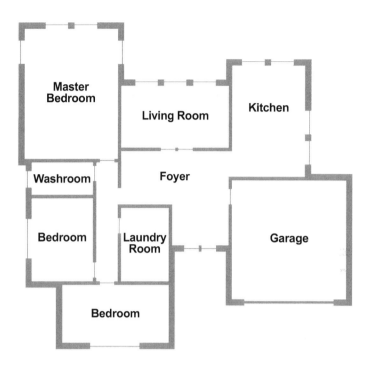

These requirements are often interlinked, in layers, like the various elements in a house:

- **Foundation:** The network or a communication subsystem that is necessary for your devices to access the internet.

- **Walls:** Boundaries that keep not only cybercriminals but also all external traffic outside your environment, as well as internal walls that act as boundaries between the various departments.

- **Electricity:** The platform your data needs to operate on (like the electricity installation in your house), ie your computers and their operating system.

- **Lighting and appliances:** Specialized software needed to access your data, such as an accounting system, an office suite or a database.

- **Roof:** What protects you when it 'rains' – usually a backup system. You may not need it to use your data, but you will surely need it if you have to recover that data.

- **Door locks:** The thing that many people forget – computer passwords and any centralized encrypting/decrypting or other data access-management system. Your keys are your corporate identity. You will most likely need to have recovered the infrastructure that manages your users' identity (for example, managed by Microsoft Active Directory) in order to have access to your company's data.

Creating enclaves and layers

An enclave is a space that is isolated, that cannot be accessed before going through some layer of security. This applies to your data in that you want a protected area to be isolated by a security boundary that is accessible only with a specific key.

Think of the architecture of a medieval castle: it consists of layer upon layer of security. The aim is to make it as hard as possible for the enemy to get to the person in authority. The drawbridge is like the separation between public and private data, which might need to be accessible only from certain sites or even certain countries. The portcullis lets in only managed and certified devices, to access confidential data – and a guard will be asking for valid credentials to prove that everyone has the right to enter the castle. To access the throne room, they will have to belong to the nobility. Nobody, but nobody, is ever given a set of all the keys.

Let's take a walking tour of the castle. I will use a scoring system as my means to let you pass through the various gates. You come to the drawbridge and show that you're not an enemy, through basic validation, say you are trusted at 10%, and you go in. You come to the portcullis, and then the guard wants you to show that you are not bringing any weapons, and you leave your sword and walk in, your score rises, and you are now at 25%. You are still far away from the throne room, and you could do minimal damage here, but someone already knows what you look like, and your major weapons have been removed. Let's try to go further. You go through the inner bailey and you move towards the castle's keep. You are stopped by two heavily armed guards, who force you to stop and identify yourself. You show a valid identification, remove your hood, and they see your face and realize that you are, in fact, their king. They fall to their knees and let you in. Your score is suddenly 100. You have access to everything, but someone else would have been stopped.

In the technology world, we score devices and users by asking and answering a series of test questions. Is this a known and managed device? Is it up to date? Is it in its known location? Has the user validated multifactor authentication? And so on. Each item adds to the working security score and adds trust to both the device and the user. If either falls below a certain level, we ask for a recertification. If it fails, it is blocked.

Each 'layer' will have added protections, such as encryption, auditing and specific security scores, to demonstrate to any cybercriminals that getting to your treasure will cost them too much effort, hence reducing the potential value of attacking you – just as a well-designed castle would have discouraged raiders in medieval times. Security scores are provided by platforms such as Microsoft Defender XDR to act as a barometer to evaluate the exposure of your data, devices, applications and identity to risk.

With that in mind, your cybersecurity system will consist of a number of layers, as follows:

- **Layer 1 (outer layer):** Low protection – hosts your public data.

- **Layer 2:** Medium protection and monitoring – hosts your confidential data.

- **Layer 3:** Higher protection, monitoring and verification – hosts your internal-only data.

- **Layer 4 (inner layer):** Hosts your restricted data.

It should now be clear why I suggested keeping the list of categories restricted. The more categories you have, the more layers this cybersecurity system will need.

Let us explore and define these protection layers:

Layer 1 (outer layer)

Since this data is meant for public use or has already been published on the internet, there is no point wasting time and energy trying to protect it. It can simply be disregarded.

Layer 2

Confidential information may not be critical to the health of the enterprise, but it is nobody's business but your own. Hence the need to set boundaries. As mentioned before, this data is loosely guarded. It should only go out to friendly partners and, while it is within our walls, we are still aware of it and are keeping an eye on it (it is monitored and audited), so it will not be stolen. The important data is under lock when not in use (this is called 'encryption at rest'). Basically, by setting these boundaries, you are telling everyone in the company that this is sensitive content: before it goes outside these walls, someone will need to approve that.

Layer 3

For internal-only data, you need to apply the same boundaries that are applicable to Layer 2, plus the following security measures:

- Secondary level of authentication (or multifactor authentication/MFA, which we'll look at later in this chapter)

- Protecting it while it is moving (this is called 'encryption in transit')

- Fully monitored usage

- Usable only on corporate devices

- Unable to save to external cloud storage or personal devices

- Blocking the ability to share outside the company

This means that, if this data comes out of your business, it will be unusable, as it will be encrypted.

You can, if you wish, introduce 'palliative measures' at this level. Say an important user is outside your network, on holiday perhaps, and has no corporate device with her but needs to access a document for an important transaction. Your system can allow secure web access from anywhere without compromising data or security. You could achieve this securely with such systems as Windows 365, which allows you to create a virtual corporate device in the cloud, which you can then assign to this user.

Layer 4

We are now in restricted territory. This means that, on top of all the protection already set up, you will need to add:

- Access to only a very limited group of users

- Access requiring approval by a second user, for example, for large money transfers

At this point, you are most likely thinking, 'How can I possibly run my business with all these restrictions?' That is where technology comes into play. A lot of these restrictions can be woven into the fabric of your processes and can be made transparent. This is a gradual process, and you will add layers of protection over time.

You will be able to train your people to use this new model, while a cybercriminal coming from the outside will trip on all these wires and set off all kinds of alarms.

Crafting a naming convention

Naming conventions ensure that there is a structure to your security measures, simplify operations and cybersecurity, and optimize manageability. Their power is often underestimated.

Consider the difference between being given an orderly list of groups that are all named according to a known, predictable structure, and being handed a list of names randomly selected by all members of your company. Which approach do you think will give you a better chance of spotting an external bad actor?

It takes some effort to craft a proper naming convention, and then an extra effort to get your teams to accept it and use it consistently. First, there is always a necessary thinking phase to create the foundation of a naming convention. You need to collect all the unique information you have at your disposal and see what would constitute the best structure.

Furthermore, a naming convention must usually cover more than just clients and projects. You need to take into account other operational elements, such as departments, internal projects, licence management, software distribution and device groups.

I like using Microsoft Excel to create naming conventions. Using the Concatenate function, you can simply input the base data and the names appear as if by magic.

You will need to create multiple versions of this naming convention, which will generate different results, which you will need to discuss with your team members, to see which will be the easiest to implement.

Do not hesitate to note down why you are choosing A over B, you will need to explain this reasoning in the next phase.

Once you think you have a perfect naming convention, it needs to be tested in the real world. There is absolutely no point in trying to enforce a standard convention. That is when it will be challenged. Some arguments will be valid, and the convention will need to be adjusted, but you must be able to make a distinction between criticisms based on personal dislike and those founded on functional weakness.

At the end of this process, which will be humbling (you have been warned), you will come out with a more integrated naming convention.

Here as an example is a naming convention I developed some years ago for a technology consulting company, running between fifty and 100 projects per year – often multiple projects per customer.

A unique identifier needed to be generated automatically for each project, and the data had to be, for compliance purposes, grouped by customer, and then by project. The choice was made to implement it using Microsoft 365 Groups, as the customers' teams were power users of Teams. The result was the following naming convention.

c-[company url]	Customer's MS 365
– [company url]@ indominus.ms	group, Teams
	– Customer's email
– /sites/[company url]	– Customer's hub site SharePoint
c-[company url]-[project id]	**Customer's project teams/site**
– [company url]-[project id]@indominus.ms	– Customer's project email
	– Customer's project site SharePoint
– /sites/[company url] -[project id]	

This meant that the consulting company ended up with a list of groups that looked like this:

MS 365 group name	Email	SharePoint site
c-abc.com	abc.com@indominus. ms	/sites/abc.com
c-abc.com-0147	abc.com-0147@ indominus.ms	/sites/abc.com-0147
c-montreal.ca	montreal.ca@ indominus.ms	/sites/montreal.ca
c-rethinkpress. com	rethinkpress.com@ indominus.ms	/sites/rethinkpress. com

As you can see, such a structure brings clarity to your environment's management and operations that will allow you to instantly spot anything not generated by the system. A bad actor attempting to create something nonstandard will therefore have a much harder time trying to hide in your environment.

Keep in mind, however, that your naming convention will be maintained by people other than you; if they do not respect it, it will never be fully implemented – which is almost worse than having no convention. All your employees therefore need to embrace it and make it their own. It will also need to be 'sold' to the user community at large.

Once the convention is live, it will also need to be closely monitored and reviewed at least monthly. Otherwise, it will degrade over time.

Identifying weaknesses

You now need to identify the potential cybersecurity weaknesses in your environment in each of the three areas of your business: people, processes and technology.

People

You should ask yourself basic questions, such as:

- Is my staff trained in cybersecurity?
- Do they know how to distinguish a phishing attack from a genuine email?
- Might they be tempted to click on a link to reset their email password?

Beyond that, do your staff have a security-first mindset?

What does that mean? Let me give you an example:

Someone walks into your offices wearing glasses and carrying a backpack and a laptop. He says he is from the IT company you regularly use and tells your receptionist that he is here to fix a computer for a member of staff who is absent. (*Yes, cybercriminals are that clever.*) The receptionist lets him into the absentee's office, he sits at the desk, opens up the computer and it logs in automatically. He asks the receptionist for the Wifi code – and if she would be kind enough to bring him a coffee with milk and two sugars. An hour later, he has finished and says goodbye to the receptionist, who asks if he wouldn't mind closing the office door behind him.

Human nature. *Exploited.*

That is why your staff must be trained to recognize *all* types of attack. Nowadays, attacks are omnichannel: they come through phone calls, emails, SMS and, sometimes, as in the example above, straight through your front door. Here are just a few – and if you don't know about them, there is a good chance that your people don't either:

- Phishing
- Malware
- Spoofing
- Infected web page / code injections
- Man-in-the-middle attack

- President's fraud

- Social engineering

- Denial of service

- Impersonation

- Insider's threat

If you are scratching your head, you know where your weaknesses are, but don't worry, we will be looking at these and other threats in the next chapter.

Bear in mind also that, with the advent of AI and generative models, the quality of these attacks is skyrocketing. Think of one of those phoney emails you get purporting to be from your bank; right now, it is easy to tell that it is a fake, but what if someone put the equivalent of 5,000 hours of work on it using AI? Then it would be a lot more difficult to discern.

Your people are your first line of defence against cyberattacks, and it is your responsibility to solidify them. We will look at how to do this in the next chapter.

Processes

Now that you have an outline of your people-related weaknesses, you can turn your attention to those that are process-based. Make a list of the processes that keep your business running. For each item on that list, ask yourself: if this disappears tomorrow, how will I be able to operate?

If you have processes that involve the exchange of data with external parties, there is a good chance this data can be intercepted and exploited. For example, say you have a process that asks a third party to collect and store all the financial data necessary to pay your customers. You have a major weakness. The third party's security could be breached and you would not even know, yet the impact on your business could be incalculable. Third-party breaches have impacted even the largest companies lately, including Microsoft.

What is more, you would likely be responsible for the disaster, as third-party service agreements often deny liability for loss or corruption of data. They may even state that your data may be hosted on a 'public' system such as Dropbox, which can be accessed without your (or your service provider's) agreement by over 200 companies for training, development or support purposes.

Your first task, then, even before you start analysing your own processes, is to make a list of your external partners and check that they are secured. Yes, this is the reason behind all those security surveys you are now receiving for those new, larger customers. They also need to make sure that their data, in your hands, remains safe.

Sometimes, processes do not even have to go outside your own walls to constitute a risk; the simple fact of handling data might put it at risk by being stored on a non-secured device or copied somewhere unsecured or downloaded for review without being properly deleted.

Mapping processes can indeed feel like herding cats, but the goal here is not to launch yourself into a full, company-wide process-analysis exercise, which would cost way too much and most likely be obsolete before the ink dried on the report, but to map the high-level processes and share them with those who are responsible for those particular processes. This will need to be a team effort as different members of different teams will need to participate in this mapping exercise. Make sure that everyone concerned is aware of and agrees with each process. Simple awareness of weaknesses and the steps that must be taken to make them secure will go a long way.

Bear in mind that it is not always your data that cybercriminals are after. I was recently at an agricultural technologies event talking to the dairy farmer I mentioned in the last chapter, who was telling me that he now used robots to collect the milk so that a team of just two farmers could manage his 1,000 cows. When I asked him whether the robots had been secured, he looked at me strangely and asked, 'What for?' My answer was simple: 'Because if they aren't, they can be taken over and they can be shut down.' Then I had a question for him: 'How much would you be prepared to pay to keep your milk flowing?'

Technology

What is the door to your information? The answer is your devices. All those devices you use to access your email, your documents or your data. They are the tools you use on a daily basis, but they are also the conduits that will be used by cybercriminals to extract your data to the dark web.

If they infiltrate a device, they can create a nest, a base within your company, and from there they can spread their influence by 'moving laterally' to other devices within the company. They can also use this device to escalate privileges, obtaining more and more access rights that allow them to dig ever deeper into your company.

When I started Indominus, we created a cybersecurity score for devices based on the Microsoft score. This told us instantly what the threat level was, by device, by platform (Windows, Apple, Android, and so on). This allowed us to know what vulnerabilities needed to be fixed and the 'patches' and fixes required.

In order to defend them properly, you need a few technologies. Here, the motto 'less is more' is required.

For years, technical architects have designed solutions using the 'best-of-breed model', which meant that they researched for the best product in a category, and this was the recommendation for that portion of the environment. This leads to technology sprawl, where you have fifty technologies for a given environment. Since 2016, with Microsoft making strides to have leading products in each category, you can now have a 'best of platform model', where you can have a normalized, standardized line of products, which are all aligned and are built to work together, hence reducing complexity and giving a deeper understanding of the overall environment.

By reducing the number of technologies and moving towards 'best of platform' as opposed to 'best of breed', you will drastically reduce any compatibility or security integration issues and simplify the overall management processes – which means better understanding and clearer focus, as well as improved confidence when it comes to using those technologies. Keeping things simple makes it both a lot more protectable and a lot more affordable. No company, in today's talent-shortage era, can afford to have a team of 100 people managing their technology stack.

Simplicity breeds deeper insight into your security environment.

Your security technologies should be acting as sensors and guard rails. Users do not need to be highly involved in that technology; in fact, the ideal scenario is one where they don't realize all that is happening in the background. Always remember that the best technology is the technology you don't see. It should make your life easier, simpler and safer, hence reducing your workload, not adding to it.

Here are the essential technologies (you are most likely already using some of them since your company is still up and running):

- Encryption

- Firewalls

- Antivirus software

- Endpoint detection and response (EDR)

- Multifactor authentication (MFA)

- Biometrics

- Twenty-four-hour monitoring

- Password vaults

- Data loss protection (DLP)

- Tagging

Again, don't worry: we will be looking in detail at these and other technologies in the next chapter.

Configurations

No matter which cloud service provider you are using, their defaults are never the proper way to be secured. Their standard configurations are there to be the most compatible, to allow the most functionalities, but they are seldomly the most secure.

For example, the default antispam policies within Microsoft 365 are not the ones that will be the harshest against spam. Why? Because Microsoft does not want first-time users complaining that they are not receiving emails.

Conversely, if you set all configurations to their safest levels, most of your employees would not be able to work. Functionalities would be blocked all over the place.

As Benjamin Franklin said: 'Those who would give up essential liberty, to purchase a little temporary safety, deserve neither liberty nor safety.' If one is willing to sacrifice fundamental freedoms for temporary security, they will ultimately lose both and deserve neither. In a cybersecurity context, this translates to: if you lock down everything, not much functionality will be left.

Before you can establish the right configurations, you should carry out a preliminary audit of your current configurations and assess your vulnerabilities. This will allow you to choose the proper configurations for your specific business.

If you are using Microsoft 365, make use of the security indicators that 'score' your various services, such as identity, apps, data and devices. Those indicators also contain useful recommendations on how to improve the security of your configurations.

Digital identity

Your digital identity is whatever is required for you to prove that you are who you say you are and gain access to your data and services online. It usually boils down to a username (or an email address) and a password. Today, with the hundreds of services, social networks and work-related online tools, most of us have multiple digital identities, but they all link back to us. What happens if they are compromised?

Someone out there can act on your behalf. If they gain access to your Facebook account, for example, they can contact all your family and friends and tell them… anything they like. They could also access all the services that you allow to be accessed with that identity.

That may be a low-impact scenario, but what if someone steals your corporate identity? What if they can now find out how much money you have in the bank? If they can order goods as if they were you? What if they could extract your corporate data to the dark web, delete your backups and then encrypt everything and leave you crippled? They could also use your identity to link in all your trusted suppliers and start doing the same thing to them.

This is how important it is to protect your identity. It is crucial. So do this exercise: whenever you type in a username and a password, take a minute to note down what that allows you to do and all that could be done if that identity was compromised. Do that for a week and this will provide you with a roadmap of your weakest and most critical identifiers.

ONE PASSWORD FOR ALL: A NIGHTMARE STORY

I used to think that having a great password was enough to protect me, and so I devised a sixteen-character password that included uppercase and lowercase letters, digits and symbols, and I used it for everything. Hundreds of potential digital identities, one password.

All that did was accelerate the speed at which my world would come to a grinding halt if that password was breached. Once they gained access to the password, Cybercriminals only had to figure out the username portion of that keyset for each service. And usernames are usually stored in clear text. It is not the portion that you are thinking about protecting.

Reflect on this for a moment: are your passwords all the same? Could a cybercriminal, from a single compromised identity, gain access to all of them? How much trouble would this land you in?

Know your enemy

In order to protect against something, or someone, you must first understand it. Let us take a look at who these people are that are now dubbed cybercriminals. There are essentially two types of cybercriminal organization: state-sponsored groups and 'commercial' groups.

State-sponsored groups

When it went to war with Ukraine, Russia launched a vast but entirely invisible cyberattack on the country's infrastructure, intended to destabilize and spread chaos, and after the official war declaration, cyberattacks were used in 'retaliation' against the countries that were supporting Ukraine.

You might think that this is a phenomenon that is limited to Russia, but Microsoft has produced a map of threat actors in the *Microsoft Digital Defense Report 2023*, which points to all kinds of other state-sponsored groups.[12]

Tracked activity:

- Nation-state actors
- Ransomware groups
- Cyber mercenaries or private sector offensive actors

• Storm-#### designations refer to emerging or developing clusters of threat activity.

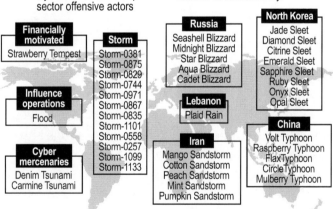

Financially motivated
Strawberry Tempest

Storm
Storm-0381
Storm-0875
Storm-0829
Storm-0744
Storm-0971
Storm-0867
Storm-0835
Storm-1101
Storm-0558
Storm-0257
Storm-1099
Storm-1133

Russia
Seashell Blizzard
Midnight Blizzard
Star Blizzard
Aqua Blizzard
Cadet Blizzard

North Korea
Jade Sleet
Diamond Sleet
Citrine Sleet
Emerald Sleet
Sapphire Sleet
Ruby Sleet
Onyx Sleet
Opal Sleet

Influence operations
Flood

Lebanon
Plaid Rain

Cyber mercenaries
Denim Tsunami
Carmine Tsunami

Iran
Mango Sandstorm
Cotton Sandstorm
Peach Sandstorm
Mint Sandstorm
Pumpkin Sandstorm

China
Volt Typhoon
Raspberry Typhoon
Flax Typhoon
Circle Typhoon
Mulberry Typhoon

As you can imagine, state actors' agendas are political and are targeted at specific groups. They seek military and economic advantages over other countries or political rivals.

You may wonder how this relates to your business – after all, you're unlikely to have an entire country as your enemy. Consider for a moment that Canada, in my universe, helps Ukraine, and that this action frustrates Russia, who chooses to retaliate against Canada. The simple fact of being a Canadian company makes my company a potential target. Again, know your enemy.

'Commercial' groups

As I have said before, we need to forget the 'teenager in a hoody in his basement' stereotype. Those teens have grown up and now run corporations that have recruiting services using social media to find the best talent and access to a whole marketplace of tools and codes designed to exploit every weakness.

First of all, it is important to understand that cyber-criminal organizations adopted remote working long before the COVID pandemic. They are a network of subcontractors and have apprentices all over the world. Once, during a cyberattack, we shut down the access point through which the attacks were being made, and our firewall showed us that they were coming from all over the world. They had spread from a single IP, in one country, to multiple different networks all over the planet, within minutes.

When responding to one incident, after some research, we found that the cybercriminals were recruiting on X (formerly Twitter). The posts looked just like normal hiring ads, with the job requirements, the pay, the profit-sharing terms, and even the hook that recruits could 'work from anywhere'. Luring people to the dark side. In plain sight.

There are essentially two types of groups, which operate in very different ways:

- Cyber-terrorists will target anyone and everyone they can find with an infected email and wait to see who clicks on it. Their goals are purely financial and they will feed off any victim, no matter what size they are. As they might say, 'It's not personal'.

- Snipers will target a specific business – usually a publicly traded company – and create the conditions to make it fail, publicly, so as to shorten its stocks. This means that they will invest months in research, finding weaknesses, infiltrating the company, figuring out its plans and strategies, and then, on the day of a big announcement, they will bring it down – and make money in the process, on top of the requested ransom.

So, as we saw in Chapter 1, you can be happily running your small business and believing that cybercriminals will not have anything to do with you, but still be a target.

Ransomware as a service

The major cybercriminal groups stopped investing in new tools and weapons of mass disruption some time ago. They are now leasing them. In other words, they have joined the 'as a service' movement. How does this work?

The group owns the major tools and codes and makes them available to its members, with instructions and commission models. Each of the team members picks what they need to do their part of the work – for example, crafting infected emails from a template, creating the actual payload (the malware that will cripple your company) that encrypts your data, building the portal that will host the ransom demand. When the victim pays, all the participants get a share, and the group gets richer.

In the various phases of an attack, cybercriminals will connect to the dark web to download toolkits, provide access to other specialists or exfiltrate data to execute 'extorsion economics' – asking for a ransom with the threat of divulging secrets, reselling intellectual property or simply exposing personal data. In other words: blackmail.

The scary part is the apprentices. Not all those localized SMS attacks that you receive on your mobile and in your email inbox come from overseas, from some foreign, remote country. A lot of them can be traced back to schools. Just as criminal gangs have been able to corrupt young people by promising them 'easy money' through drug reselling and other criminal activities, the dark web has started seducing them into cyber criminality. Now, instead of handling cocaine and heroin on the street, they sit at home emptying retirees' accounts and come to school the following week with a luxury car and a false identity – all by-products of cyber criminality.

This aspect of cybercrime is going to become less and less popular now that large insurance companies have announced that they will no longer pay ransoms, but for the time being, it is very much a fact of business life.

Know your score

You need to be in a position to score your cybersecurity posture. I have created a tool for online evaluation that allows you to know where you stand.

It will take you through the SECURE model, and will ask you:

- How well you have mastered your *Survey*?

- How *Educated* are you, your management team and your staff?

- What did you *Construct* for your defences?

- Have you *Unified* your security?

- How often do you *Review* your security plan and controls?

- How do you make sure your strategy *Evolves* over time?

After completing the survey of your own landscape and the world of cyber criminality, how important is it for you, as a business owner, to know what your 'SECURE score' is?

 This free online test will let you know, within twenty minutes, exactly where you stand. If your score is good, then well done, although there is almost always more that can be done. If your score is low, the advice in this book will help you make your business secure. When you have made improvements, try the test again.

You can access the test at: https://bulletin.indominus.ms/areyouSECURE.

Summary

In order to protect something, you must first know what you are protecting and against what you are protecting it from. The first task is to identify your important data and services and classify them so that you can prioritize their security. This allows you to apply the appropriate level or layer of security to each, as well as giving you greater clarity on what to do in the event of an incident.

It is also important to understand the nature of the enemy – how they operate and what their motivations are. This allows you to start working out how they might attack you, and what they might be after.

Be efficient in protecting. Not everything needs to survive a cyberattack, but make sure that whatever does need to survive is adequately protected.

Your cybersecurity score will tell you how well you are doing in the various aspects of your company's cybersecurity so that you know what to focus on next.

THREE

Educate

Everyone in your company, from the senior management team down to the individual employees, should be aware of the need for cybersecurity and understand their role in maintaining it at all times. But, when it comes to cybersecurity, the buck stops with you. If a cyberattack is launched from within your premises, as is increasingly the case, and it can be traced back to your equipment, you can be held criminally accountable.

So, before enrolling anyone else in your new cybersecurity culture, you yourself must have an idea of what you are talking about.

Educate yourself

Do you feel ill-equipped to become the epicentre of a wave of human change within your organization? Do your staff think they don't need change management? If so, keep in mind the words of Geneviève Desautels, founder of multiple start-ups and one of the most interesting speakers on change management:

> 'Put "human" at the centre of any changes.
> Empower your people to embrace the
> change as something that is going to enhance
> their potential.'

Understanding this is the cornerstone of any successful change within a culture because people won't change unless they want to. Even under duress. If they are convinced that what they are doing is the right thing to do, they will keep on doing it – until they realize that another way will benefit them. The first thing to do is to make a plan.

Now that you have surveyed your environment and have a map of your important data and systems, you need to start planning how you will secure them if something terrible does happen – whether a cyberattack or a pandemic – to make sure that your business keeps going. For this, you need a plan.

Start by asking yourself: who will need to change in order to make this data and those services more secure? What will they (and I) need to know to be effective? How will this make their life better?

If you aren't already, you will need to start being curious as to how your most precious assets can be protected, what tools and techniques are available to you and how effective they might be in your particular landscape. This doesn't mean that you have to become a cybersecurity expert, but you will need to invest some time in understanding at least the basics, and then surround yourself with people who know more than you do on the subject.

As the person responsible for your customers' and employees' information, you will need to be familiar with a few concepts:

- **Vendor security:** Do you have any partners, vendors or subcontractors with whom you share data? How secure are they? If you provide them with sensitive information, is it secured? Your responsibility does not end with the sale of your goods or services; you need to make sure data stays safe. How? Surveying your business partners will help you add SECURE criteria to your vendor selection process.

- **Legal liability:** Do the laws that apply to your company also apply to your supply chain? If you take your customers' data, or personal information, and put it in Dropbox or pass it through Zapier, what is your liability? What does your master service agreement say (or did you simply click 'I accept' without giving it any thought)? Someone in your company will need to look at all these agreements and contracts and evaluate your risks.

- **Data protection:** While this sensitive data lies within your company, what do you do to keep it secure? Are the processes, people and technology aligned to keep it secure? Do you have any controls that make sure you can trace who uses it and whether it has been shared externally? Note that, if you answered 'no' a few times, that is normal. If you are suddenly worried, that is normal too. When you start putting the proper value on data, you have to start protecting it, and no, that does not mean simply backing it up, but starting to consider that it is the lifeblood of your company. If someone steals it or corrupts it or simply stops you from being able to access it, you need to know the impact and what you need to do to protect it.

- **Regulatory compliance:** What are the regulations you must comply with? If you are handling card payments, you may be subject to the PCI standard. If you are in healthcare, you might, in the US, be bound by legislation such as the Health Insurance Portability and Accountability Act. Once you have identified all the relevant regulations, you will need to find out what their requirements for data security, confidentiality and handling are.

- **User responsibilities and contractual agreements:** When you provide an employee with a computer, a network and access to the internet, that does not make it their personal device – it is still the company's hardware and software, and the company is ultimately responsible for whatever they do with it. If, for example, an employee decides to install an illegal version of AutoCAD to 'play around with' and the company is audited for software licence compliance, you will have to pay for those licences, plus penalties and potentially a lawsuit for breaking the law. If one of your employees lets his teenager use your computer at night to play games and she gets bored and decides to go out and explore the dark web… In all such scenarios, the buck stops with you. Most likely, all your employees are adults. As such, they understand the binding nature of an agreement, of their signature – in theory. It is important that you, as CEO, remind them of their responsibilities.

As we have said, all these are ultimately your responsibility and should therefore be covered in your cyber-security plan.

Now that you have a plan, it's time to look at some of the technical considerations involved in implementing it. You might not be the technical type, but, again, you must master the basics – even if you are going to hire an expert to put your plan into action. Here are some of the terms you should be familiar with.

Firewalls

The firewall is the gate and fence to your land. It validates everyone who wants to go in or out, and guards the door to the outside world. Each time you allow a new software to communicate to the internet, it pokes a hole in that door. Eventually, if you aren't careful, there can be more holes than door protecting your entrance. It basically raises a fence around your lot, creating a perimeter of protection between your world and the external jungle known as the internet.

A firewall is a requirement as soon as you have an office or a building that you need to protect. This creates a barrier and filters everything that comes in and out of your site. (In fact, as explained below, a firewall is basically a vast quantity of rules that allow you to restrict who can access what.)

A firewall is critical in linking sites together if you have more than one. It will also enable you to create a secured connection to a data centre or virtual (cloud) data centre, and it will allow your remote users to connect to the office securely via an encrypted channel called a virtual private network (VPN) – see below.

If properly configured, a firewall can include such properties such as blocking specific countries, filtering outgoing traffic and recording what is happening, so that you can be warned if something unusual happens.

The primary goal of a firewall, historically, was to keep people out, and it used to be the ultimate solution in security. This stopped being the case with the advent of phishing emails in the early 2000s, enabling cybercriminals to launch attacks from within companies' networks, so that a firewall now has to protect the company even against its own devices.

When you talk to the person responsible for setting up and monitoring your firewall, check that the following steps will be taken:

- Block *any access* to the dark web

- Log and validate outgoing traffic

- Block suspicious countries

- Make sure that all rules have been validated and that:

  - Not a single rule has all ports opened

  - Not a single rule gives access to all machines from outside

  - You have a distinct approval process for incoming rules, especially those that go far and wide (lots of machines, exposed to a large external audience)

The firewall can also host a VPN. A VPN creates a privacy tunnel, which is totally encrypted, between two firewalls. Those tunnels can be used to link two sites or allow a device to remotely connect to a corporate site, allowing users to work remotely, just as if they were in the office.

If you are running an office without a firewall, you should be aware that any device roaming on your network is fully exposed to the internet, and any weakness can be exploited from anywhere in the world without even raising an alarm.

Nevertheless, although a firewall will keep most threats at bay, it is no longer the focal point of a cybersecurity system. It remains a critical part of tracing back attacks when investigating.

Endpoints

You might wonder why I am starting with endpoints. The reason is that, not only are they the most vulnerable part of your environment, but they are also the most used. They host your users' credentials (identity) and, if someone wants to extract data from your network, the endpoints will be the easiest way to access it.

So how can you protect your endpoints? There are a few ways to do this.

Encryption

You don't want to leave your data exposed to anyone on the internet. In order to do that, you must protect it. This is your first level of protection. Encryption will take your data and make it unusable without the proper key. That key is bound to your identity. This means that, for you, as long as you are authenticated, it will be transparent. If someone else comes along and wants to access your file, they won't be able to understand what it is as it will be scrambled.

Endpoint-level firewall

Just like you can protect your perimeter with a firewall, your laptop and desktop can have a miniature replica of the service, protecting your endpoint against more direct attacks. This is useful if you are working say from an airport, a hotel room or a café, using public, unprotected Wifi.

Antivirus

Computer viruses are just like their human counterparts: they attack parts of your systems and cause damage – sometimes minor, sometimes fatal. An antivirus will act like your body's immune system and, just like the latter, will only block and quarantine what it recognizes. It is now considered a basic tool, but it is still an important layer of protection.

Endpoint detection and response (EDR)

EDR is the evolution of antivirus software. The major difference is that, instead of relying on a library of known virus definitions, it looks for patterns and behaviours. If an antivirus acts like a vaccinated immune system programmed to fight specific and known viruses, EDR is like the immune system's innate immunity – able to recognize a wide range of unidentified threats. When it catches a device (endpoint) doing something it knows to be either dangerous or detrimental, it isolates the process. EDR will also look for vulnerabilities, identifying where malware might take advantage of your device's configuration.

EDR is a smoke detector, it will let you know the moment something is wrong, and, just as you must keep the batteries in your smoke detectors charged, it is vital to make sure that your devices are connected to the internet and able to receive regular updates.

EDR itself is now a base technology. XDR, the extended version, usually includes background automation so that it reacts automatically to specific events, and MDR is the managed version, usually by a managed security service provider (MSSP).

NB: An EDR solution generates tons of information. If you don't have a qualified analyst at the receiving end, you are still a few steps behind cybercriminals and you will not see them coming.

Security updates, drivers and patches

Just as bugs are found and fixed in new versions of software, your operating system is tested daily for new weaknesses. That is why the various levels of updates should be done at least monthly, to make sure that all base vulnerabilities have been fixed.

Servers

Servers are the next step in the chain of your cybersecurity strategy.

Servers can live in three realities: physical, virtual and cloud. The physical server, hosted on your premises, has been purchased and is managed by your team. Then, perhaps down the road, someone in the team figured out that you could buy fewer, bigger servers and partition them, hosting virtual servers. Then you can choose to do away with physical servers and move those virtual machines to the cloud, where the hardware will be managed by someone else, and you will retain management of your virtual server.

Servers are divided into three main components: the hardware, the operating system and the actual application they are servicing. For example, you may buy a machine that is hosting an operating system (Windows) to run your CRM (Dynamics 365).

All three of these components can be attacked and, therefore, must be maintained and monitored.

You might be thinking, 'You can't attack hardware', but in order to function properly, hardware requires specialized pieces of code known as firmware and drivers; if those are out of date or contain weaknesses, they can be used to disrupt or attack your business.

Your operating system can also be targeted through various weaknesses, which, if not properly patched, become holes through which cybercriminals can gain access to obtain credentials, disrupt or use as a base to launch their next level of attack. That next attack may well be designed to extract your data or listen to every key you type on your keyboard.

The greatest risk lies with your identity servers. If you are still hosting on-premises servers, your active directory servers (the servers that manage your identity and authenticate everyone – sometimes referred to as domain controllers) are the most vulnerable, and access to them is the fastest way for criminals to cripple your entire company because they can then prevent anyone from authenticating anything. You must protect them at all costs. As a bonus, they would get access to everyone's identity.

This is one of the reasons why system administrators have always deployed active directory servers in groups of two or more, to ensure that the data it contains would not be lost. That has also given those servers a special status within companies making them 'untouchables', which sometimes equates to *no one wants to touch them*. This created another problem, because the servers tend to get obsolete and filled with objects that are no longer used and no one is taking care of. This is opening tons of backdoors that cybercriminals can use.

There are two sides to this problem. First, it's a highly stable technology. It has evolved since its inception in February 2000 – nearly a quarter of a century ago. It is a rock. On the other side, it has become so central, such a cornerstone of identity and security, that most system administrators do not want to touch it. It scares them, and some administrators forget them all together as a result. Imagine the weaknesses that accumulate over years of neglect.

Microsoft created a cloud equivalent, the Azure Active Directory (recently renamed *Entra*), which is less susceptible to attacks but still not inviolable.

Services

Services are what keep your business running. You may never have heard of SMTP, but without this service, it would be impossible for anyone to send an email. However, although critical, SMTP is ageing. By default, it requires only a username and password for an email to be sent. No modern authentication or MFA. What does that do for your security? It creates a weakness begging to be exploited.

And this is just one of many services your company relies on – all of which you need to assess and, ultimately, secure.

Those services are in the background, you never hear of them, but here are a few examples:

- **NTP (Network Time Protocol):** This is used to keep all the servers and devices synced. A crucial, yet invisible service.

- **SNMP:** Used to transmit the state of the various servers and receive commands at the operational backend level.

- **FTP(s) (File Transfer Protocol):** Used to transfer files over the internet. The S stands for its secured and encrypted edition.

- **HTTP(s) (Hypertext Transfer Protocol):** Used to create the exchange of data across the internet. It is the transport protocol for every website in the world.

- **SMB (Server Message Block):** Used for file exchange in a Windows network.

The issue is that most of these services date back to the 90s and even earlier for some of them, leaving them plagued with vulnerabilities. Since their adoption is so wide, reforming and evolving them is of the highest complexity.

SMB is the perfect example, the original version is a security nightmare, full of holes. Its current implementation, version 3, is considered secure, but its deployment is complex due to backward compatibility.

Digital identity

In the last chapter, we saw the vital importance of protecting your digital identity. The question now is, how? There are a few solutions you should implement as soon as possible:

Multifactor authentication (MFA)

MFA is a technology that adds a layer of complexity to compromising an account. A classic example is the verification codes that are sent to your phone. Without access to your phone as well, no one can access your data.

Password vault

Vaults are a great concept. Just like the vault in your bank, they are secured by the vendor but inaccessible to them. The content, and the key, belong to you. They integrate everything (phone, browser, Windows) and they capture every request for a password. Whether you are subscribing to a new online service, registering for points with an airline or signing in to your personal email, it all gets captured. Another benefit is that you can link a private and a professional profile, allowing you to stay secure in both your work and personal life.

Perhaps the best thing about vaults is that they generate new, totally random passwords for each service you use. They also autofill usernames and passwords, which stops you from needing to type your password every time. Cybercriminals often use a tool known as a key logger, which logs all the keystrokes you make on your keyboard, so every time your password vault fills in a password for you, there is one less chance of that password being compromised.

Even though the cloud keeps multiple copies of your important documents and communications, some documents need special protection. Much like your will and your insurance papers, these should therefore be stored in a vault or safe somewhere outside your corporate infrastructure.

Biometrics and passwordless technology

Biometrics is the technology that allows you to use part of your body as an identity factor. Instead of typing a password, a sensor might recognize your face or your fingerprint and use this as a password instead. Passwordless technology is aiming more towards tokens and digital identity cards that allow you to demonstrate who you are, just like you would when you are voting or boarding a flight.

Backups

As I am sure you are aware, backups are your ultimate recovery tool. If you do not have a valid copy of your data somewhere in the event of a ransomware attack, you are as good as dead. As we saw in Chapter 1, you might think that, if you have a cloud-based backup, this is all you need, but this is merely a first-level safety net that ensures that data can be retrieved rapidly if you delete it by mistake – though when you consider telecommunication link speeds, a cloud backup can be anything but efficient.

An effective backup system might consist of the following:

- A physical copy of key contacts, including:
  - A trusted IT subcontractor that you have previously contacted to recover systems and data
  - Your backup service provider
  - A lawyer specialized in cybercrime

- – A list of shareholders and partners

- – A public relations / crisis-management firm to manage the reputational impact of a cyberattack

- Updated laptops outside the corporate network

- Invoicing and payroll data in separate cloud services

- An on-demand office space with network access and a printing facility

- A physical copy of all relevant data in a safe outside your offices

- A printed plan of your services and processes – note that this needs to be a living document that is kept up to date as the months go by

There are a few important things to do when considering what to back up where and how:

- As discussed in Chapter 2, you should secure the various data types in accordance with their criticality; there is no point backing everything up, as your backup will rapidly become unusable.

- Try to keep your data in the same location or within a few hours of delivery if you are using an off-site service. The idea here is the velocity of recoverability. How fast can you get back online?

- Make sure that your backup system is clean. This might seem obvious, but you would be surprised how many backups we have had to restore because they were infected with another version of the problem we were trying to resolve.

- Check that whoever is providing you with your backup service is trustworthy, make sure that your contract with them is properly reviewed, and test the service to ensure that it is reliable.

Data loss protection (DLP)

Data extraction has become a fact of life, especially since the pandemic. Everyone in your company, perhaps even you, has brought documents home on an external storage device (or USB stick) because you didn't feel like carrying the laptop. With the pandemic, the number of 'bypasses' that were put in place to enable people to work from home was astronomical and the potential security impacts are nothing short of nightmarish.

DLP can be described as the security camera of your cyber-defence strategy. It monitors and records all that happens to your data. It prevents access to sensitive data, so that only the intended audience can read it, and it can trigger alerts, enable encryption and isolate data when a breach or other security incident is detected.

If a criminal tries to open a confidential document that you have protected with DLP outside your environment, they will be asked to identify themselves. Since they won't be able to do so, the document will be unusable. It's like if you had educated your data on the art of Kung Fu. It knows how to defend itself.

Furthermore, you will be able to tell who tried to open it and when. With perimeter protection (discussed later in this chapter), you can also know where it was taken from – though if your perimeter defences were properly configured, you might have stopped it from leaving in the first place.

Insider threat

As we have seen, insider threats are insidious. By default, an employee is a person you trust, so protecting against them is unnatural. Nevertheless, this is where a lot of data exfiltration originates from. Disgruntled or angry former employees, staff that are being blackmailed or coerced, or simply people that are careless… there are many ways that your data can end up on the dark side.

The first thing to do, then, is to be suspicious. If a member of staff – especially one that you know is unhappy about some aspect of their work – asks for company or customer information that they wouldn't normally need or attempts to gain access to privileged data, you should ask them why and make sure that any information they are granted access to is suitably protected.

If, however, they are intent on misusing data that they already have access to, it may be difficult to prevent them, although you can ensure that you are warned if the volume exceeds what is normal.

This is where you have to provide *just-enough* privilege versus an all-open approach. It is better for privilege to be given *à la pièce*, rather than all or nothing.

Tagging

Tagging is like barcoding: it allows you to keep an inventory of all your data and to know what is where. More importantly, it enables you to classify everything accurately. During your initial survey, you will have created buckets in which you classified your data. Now, each time you create a new piece of content, you can simply attach predefined tags, allowing it to be automatically placed in the proper container. Then it will automatically be properly protected.

When you add tags (also known as metadata) to a piece of data, you are also enriching it, thereby helping a search engine to find it. In fact, tagging is the reason we can find anything almost instantly on the internet. Every single website published is marked with content tags that tell search engines what it contains, who its audience is and whether or not it is safe for children.

For example, first I create a document and I name it *Company ABC*. Then I enrich it with the following tags:

- Document type: Business proposal

- Customer: Company ABC

- Object: Initial CRM deployment

- Description: Initial landing – Europe

- Sensitivity: Highly confidential

- Audience: Executives

With those six tiny pieces of information, your data loss protection (DLP) system is automatically aware of the highly sensitive nature of this document.

Logging and auditing

Considering that DLP is your security camera, auditing is like your security personnel looking at the footage. Now, since there can be millions of interactions in a day, consider that all those actions are extracted and translated into text so that you can search them.

One of the rules of any cyber-defence strategy is trace-ability – the ability to find out what happened in the event of any security breach, and to reconstruct the story of what happens in an investigation. Auditing allows you to trace your company's data and services.

It allows you, either during or after an event, to figure out what has happened. It allows you, usually, to find out who took which actions and when, and what objects were affected. It can become as complex as having a complete trace of all chats that an employee has had over the past year.

Why do this? Do we have a big brother complex? The quick answer is no, but, as the business owner, you are both liable and responsible. If something happens on company grounds, ultimately, you are responsible for it. You're the captain. From that point of view, how well-armed do you want to be if someone comes at you with a lawsuit saying that your company stole one of their secrets or attempted to tarnish their reputation? At that point, you will want to know exactly who said what to whom, with the full context available for review.

That is one of the reasons why auditing exists.

You can't keep track of all interactions within your company's environment, as that would rapidly become unusable and expensive. You need to have access to the cases that stood out, that raised an eyebrow. If you need to track everything whether it raises eyebrows or not, you can always put in place a secondary, less-expensive, archive storage that will allow you to go back in time.

Here are a few of the other reasons why logging and auditing should be turned on by default. Filtered yes, so they don't cost you a fortune in storage, but most definitely not *off*:

- **Track user activity:** No, I am not talking about tracking what your users are doing by the minute to find out if they are productive! How dare you think something like that? I am referring to whether they are accessing only what they should or are they trying to access systems/data that they are not supposed to.

- **Mitigate risk:** Cyberattacks nowadays are complex creatures. They come in multiple, small, calculated steps. One of the great developments of today's tools is that, in the backend, they are actually validating those steps and can, through auditing, find correlation, and stop a cybercriminal's initial steps.

- **Identify who's attempting to invade your property:** As mentioned before, the way to get to your piece of land is through a gatekeeper, your firewall. What has the firewall got to do with auditing? That is the beauty of auditing, it will source its data from multiple sources, including firewalls. The idea is that each service contributes, creating a trail of bread crumbs in the event of a security breach.

A SMALL ENGINEERING FIRM, SOMEWHERE IN QUEBEC

We receive a call in the middle of the day, 'We've been hacked, it's ransomware, we have been trying to recover for four days... can you help?'

Within a few hours, we are setting up a war room in their conference room. The first thing we do is take over the firewall, the literal gate to their environment.

My partner, Sylvain Gagner,* starts looking at the logs and rewrites part of the configuration, and within a few minutes, he tells me: 'They are coming from about twenty countries. As soon as we closed the door by which they were passing, we saw attempts coming from all over the place.'

How did he know? *Auditing.*

Through the various attempts to access the system, the firewall created a complete log, an audit of all actions taken. Once deciphered, we were able to know where the attacks came from.

And this is only the first byte of that story – more to come later.

---

*   Sylvain Gagner is a firewall guru. I met him at Bombardier Aerospace and I completely respect his encyclopaedic knowledge of firewalls and networking.

Email messaging

Messaging can be used in multiple ways to compromise your business, your finances and, ultimately, your data. Implementing security measures to defend yourself against these cyberattacks is therefore essential. Over 80% of the time, email is the means used by cybercriminals to infiltrate networks, systems and devices. Most ransomware attacks are initiated through email.

The email system as we know it today has not changed much since its popularization in the second half of the 90s. It was designed to allow the flow of messages from and to anywhere on the planet. It was built to enable high volumes of messages and speedy delivery. It was never intended to be filtered and protective. As we shall see in the next chapter, various companies have contributed to improving the base protocols of email messaging systems, but additions are hard to implement as they are so varied and widespread.

So how do cybercriminals take advantage of your messaging systems? Here are the best-known messaging methods they use.

Phishing emails

This is usually a well-crafted email that invites you to click on a link. It may purport to be from your bank, a delivery service or any other service that you habitually use. The goal is simple: to get you to give away some information.

For example, a typical phishing email that appears to come from your bank will tell you that there is either a deposit awaiting your approval or that your account has been compromised, and instructs you to 'click here' to reset your password. The website you are taken to might also start deploying some malware onto your device, but the ultimate goal is to collect personal information such as your bank or credit card number and password – not only in order to empty your bank account, but also to resell your personal details. Like any cyberattack, as we have seen, such emails can be part of a 'blanket' onslaught (bulk phishing) or a targeted attack (spear phishing).

The simplest thing to do is to check whether the email domain is right. For example, if your bank is the Royal Bank of Canada, and the email domain ends with .cn instead of .ca, you know that it has come from somewhere in China and is therefore highly unlikely to be genuine. With the evolution of AI and large-language models, long gone are the days where you could spot a phishing email due to the number of grammatical errors it contained. You now need to be extra careful, validating that the links included direct to the proper address of the company mentioned (for example, by hovering your mouse on top of the link). If it doesn't, this is a red flag. Other giveaways may include the email signature name not matching the email address it was sent from. In the case of phishing emails, you need to be extra careful – better safe than sorry.

Malware

Malware is a contraction of 'malicious software' and does exactly what it says. Also known as the 'initial payload', it is used to compromise the device on which it is opened and establish the command centre from which to launch an invasion.

Digital hygiene and being careful are your most efficient weapons against it. You need to make sure that whatever you download and install is genuine and not weaponized, falsified software. Antivirus software can be used to scan any files for known malware before it is downloaded or installed, and tools are available that can clean up your device once malware is installed, but these are insidious pieces of software and can be difficult to remove. An EDR will also stop it from deploying. These two form a pair that will stop most malware from installing.

Once the first piece of malware is deployed on your device, seventy-two minutes is all it takes a cyber-criminal to compromise it.[13] At that point, they will have embedded themselves within your device and will be ready to spread their destruction to the rest of your company. Without the proper monitoring, they can lay dormant for months within your business, collecting information and spreading their reach.

Password spray attack

Let's compare this attack to a squirt from a can of hair spray. It sends millions of droplets across a wide area. That is what a *spray attack* does. It attempts millions of passwords, over a long period of time and from multiple vectors. This means that security systems cannot detect the attack. Rather than using brute force (trying millions of passwords, rapidly, on a single username), it is attempting multiple passwords on numerous users, from multiple diverse locations. If successful, this will give the cybercriminals access to legacy services such as SMTP (Simple Mail Transfer Protocol) or IMAP (Internet Mail Access Protocol), which will allow them to send emails on the user's behalf and initiate 'official' emails without the need for MFA, thereby bypassing any second level of authentication.

Man-in-the-middle (MITM)

This type of attack is also known as an injection and involves someone hijacking your communications between your computer and, say, your bank's website. The idea is to then take over the conversation, or sometimes just to eavesdrop and listen to what is happening.

Here are a few of the most renowned MITM attacks:

Email hijacking: This is used to access your email, thereby gaining access to your communications and, for example, gathering information about upcoming corporate events or the company in general. You can push it further, though, and imitating a person's writing and linguistic style is all a well-organized cybercriminal group needs to simulate a formal email from you, that could infect or misdirect your entire company and partners.

Wifi eavesdropping: What if I could deploy a second Wifi network, with the same ID as yours, and then have all your corporate devices connect to it instead of your corporate one? Well, if there are no watchers, I can collect information for months without being bothered.

DNS spoofing: This one is a bit more technical. As you may know, a DNS (or Domain Name Server) is the internet's Yellow Pages directory. Through a worldwide architecture, it is able to find the actual address (IP address) of a given published service. For example, when you type 'www.indominus.ms', it is able to find the actual address of this website.

DNS spoofing means that a cybercriminal introduces a rogue DNS server for a given network, and makes a service believe that, for example, the email domain for Indominus is not at address A but address B. They can then start sending emails as Indominus.ms, without any constraint.

You are now able to send spam, on someone's behalf, without constraint.

This can be circumvented by setting up secure DNS services as well as ensuring that official encryption keys exist for the various services, including email and websites.

Session hijacking: This is where a cybercriminal invites themselves to a session. For example, when you authenticate with your bank, that creates a secure session, and if you leave your browsers opened in the background and someone is with you in that session, they will have access to all the actions that you have access to. You can just imagine what might happen next.

SSL hijacking: Similar to session hijacking, but this time the cybercriminal invites themselves into the actual encrypted tunnel and listens. This may be a lower-level interaction, but can enable just as damaging actions.

President's fraud

A president's fraud is a *social engineering* type of attack, which means that it will rely on human nature to succeed. Such attacks rely on first gaining internal intelligence. To do so, the bad actor must have access either to one of the leaders' identities or to their computer, or it will already have access to internal data about the company. In this respect, we can consider a president's fraud a secondary attack.

Let us imagine for a moment that you are the president of a multinational corporation and you have an assistant, Mindy, who helps you keep the business running. She is your trusted right hand. She receives an email from you saying, 'Hi Mindy, We are in the final round of negotiating for the acquisition of XYZ, Inc. I need to accelerate the negotiation and have asked our lawyers to create an incentive for the seller. Please transfer $100,000 to the lawyers; here is their banking information. Please do this ASAP as we are attempting to seal the deal today.'

Being the efficient assistant that she is, Mindy instantly complies and, boom, $100,000 disappears from your bank account, never to be seen again.

Here are the steps by which such an attack will usually take place:

- **Identification:** This is basically target acquisition – looking for a person within a well-established company, usually a new CFO or executive assistant.

- **Contact:** The target is contacted either through email or voice, pretending to be a person of authority, like the president of the company being purchased or a lawyer in the acquisition process.

- **Deception:** This is where the social engineering techniques come in, creating a sense of urgency, with tight deadlines, and applying pressure. This should be a clear warning signal – the *act now, don't think!* type of request.

- **Payment:** If it is not stopped, then the attack concludes when the funds are transferred.

Some of the most effective attacks are partially based on truth. This example above is based on a real case in which the acquisition was real and the assistant knew about it. The lawyers' account and the request for an immediate transfer were not.

The two most effective defence methods against this type of attack are a) awareness and training, so your staff is aware that this type of fraud exists, and b) a clear verification workflow – when anything is uncertain, take steps to verify it. That way, before clicking send, there is a verification phone call. Attack trumped.

Account takeover

This happens when a bad actor is able to take over your digital identity. This means that he can order on your behalf, alter your passwords, access your services and your data. It also means that he can request actions to be taken on your behalf.

Basically, living your online life. Imagine the potential damage.

Connected objects

When it comes to cybersecurity, connected objects are well-disguised villains. They are pervasive throughout our lives but have the potential to be greatly disruptive.

Consider for a moment all the connected devices that are used by your company that you might not suspect could poison or disrupt your operations:

- Printers

- Thermostats, heaters and AC

- Cameras

- Television

- Games consoles

- Connected cars / transport / logistics

- Robots

- Connected manufacturing gear

- Sensors

- Magnetic cards / door-locking systems

This is not an exhaustive list, so you will need to go through *all* your devices and systems and ask yourself how disruptive it would be if they suddenly 'failed'. What if, for example, your door-locking system kept everyone locked out of the office?

Securing the perimeter

As mentioned above, if you have an office or different sites, you must protect them just as you would a building or land that you own. You need to have a fence around it so that cyber criminals do not use it as a base.

As explained before, your firewall acts as your perimeter fence and main gate. It has rules to check what is allowed to come in or out, and it has sensors, should someone try to jump the fence.

Obviously, however, the perimeter cannot be completely sealed or no one would be able to access the internet at all. So how does this work?

The entire internet works on a protocol known as TCP/IP. Translated into plain English, this means that everything has an address and an apartment number. When you ask to go, for example, to a website, the address is returned, and depending on the service you ask, will tell your device which protocol. For example, www.indominus.ms would translate to a specific address, and https would tell me which apartment. In this case, apartment 443 for https.

As mentioned above, a firewall is basically a vast number of rules that allow you to control who can access what. The depth and width of a rule are determined by three factors: how many machines are exposed by the rule, how many ports are opened, and how many addresses, outside of your network, are allowed to go through that rule. Things get complicated over time as numerous rules either counteract each other or start opening too wide a breach, allowing for bad actors to crawl through – a so-called Swiss cheese configuration.

NB: Remember that we discussed the importance of logging for the purposes of monitoring and investigating. A firewall is one of the key components of this. Make sure that your traffic is logged, both incoming and outgoing. Also, make sure that all access to the dark web is prohibited.

Monitoring

Since cyberattacks can come from anywhere in the world, at any time, you need 24/7 monitoring. To achieve this internally, you might need between three and six extra staff (and with the current talent shortage, you might have a hard time finding them).[14] The answer is to use an external alarm monitoring service – just as you might for a house alarm. After all, there is no use in having an alarm if there is no one there to hear it. Similarly, there is no point in protecting your devices, tagging your content and putting audits in place if not a single soul ever checks anything.

Since break-ins and cyberattacks don't all happen at once, monitoring services are able to keep an eye on multiple businesses with a skeleton crew. Make sure, however, that they are experts in cybersecurity. For example, your *managed service provider* which has serviced you over the past ten years, might monitor your devices, but that does not mean that they can identify a threat, research it and hunt down whomever is trying to attack you. That requires a different skillset.

Engage your executive team

Now that you are aware of the cybersecurity risks your company faces and of the tools that are required to protect it, it is time to get your management team on board. This isn't simply a matter of telling them what needs to happen; you must first convince them that it is necessary so that they have something to rally around.

Engage them in the conversation

Cybersecurity has to become part of the conversation. It can no longer be swept under the rug so that it comes as a surprise to your management team. You could, of course, simply give each of them a copy of this book (not a bad strategy), but really you need to percolate the information it contains.

As you will quickly come to realize, the poking-about you have been doing during your survey will already have been raising eyebrows among your managers (and staff). Satisfy their curiosity and enlighten them as to what you have been looking for.

Make them accountable

First, you need to make everyone accountable for their own cybersecurity. Ask each of them to calculate the financial impact of their department being hit by ransomware. Some of them may not be able to imagine such a scenario, so ask them to assume that:

- All of the company's computers are shut down and cannot be accessed

- All production equipment is unavailable – even mechanical equipment may be dependent on a computer-connected device

- All access to cloud services is blocked

They must bear in mind that they will still need to pay their staff's salaries but without any productivity. Then ask them to factor in the cost of lost customer deliveries and the inability to bill customers or collect payments from them. What would be the cost per day? Make that a month. Finally, add to that the cost of (global) crisis management, lawyers and IT experts to attempt recovery. This number becomes your justification for 'snooping around' and imposing a cybersecurity plan.

Your managers' accountability doesn't end there, though. Each of them must also realize that any one of the suppliers, subcontractors or service providers they are in close contact with is a potential 'entry point' for cyber criminals.

They need to ask those suppliers to answer a simple survey showing how well-protected they are:

- Are they being audited yearly?

- Are their devices protected?

- Is their messaging system protected?

- Are they monitoring their cybersecurity systems?

- Are they insured?

- What are they liable for (according to their contract with your company)?

Why? Simple: you don't want to do all this cybersecurity work just for a new client to open the door and let in all kinds of strangers. As Microsoft found out with the infamous SolarWinds incident, your partners have to be at least as secure as you are.[15]

Create metrics that matter

As business leaders, we are all fully aware that whatever is not measured does not get any better. That is why I propose that you set up KPIs that will allow you to monitor your management team's progress.

To create what is known as a *baseline,* you will need to complete the following list of events:

- Departmental cybersecurity audits completed

- Service providers audited (% completed)

- Employee onboarding (% completed)

- Employee cybersecurity training (% completed)

- Protected devices (% completed)

- Any breaches or security incidents

This is the initial effort, which will need to be updated either monthly or yearly depending on the event. The recurrence will be further explained in Chapter 6.

You might consider this a little extreme, but here is an excerpt from Bill 25, recent legislation in Quebec made effective in September 2022. The UK, US or EU equivalents are still being written at the time of publication. It could easily be treated as a child of GDPR, the EU privacy law protection.

'Any cybersecurity incident that is not reported exposes the company to a liability of up to 4% of its revenue or 25 million dollars. Furthermore, all companies are required to maintain a complete log of all data breaches which can be audited at any time by the government. Any data breach is to be divulged immediately to the authorities.'[16]

Empower your staff

Your staff may be your most valuable asset, but they are also potentially the weakest link when it comes to security. You will need to invest in training them.

At the beginning of this chapter, I quoted Geneviève Desautels, who said that 'human' should be at the centre of any change. What this implies is that they must be informed of the changes as they occur. Here is a simple checklist you can use as a guide:

- Explain the reasons for each change

- Communicate the plan, covering each milestone

- Share your wins and losses, because technology projects seldom go perfectly

- Survey them

- Establish feedback channels

Being transparent with your employees will not only reduce objections, dissatisfaction and opposition to the changes, but also – if you do it right – create supporters, champions and ambassadors at all levels within your company. You should identify these people and nurture and train them because they will be your first line of defence: if anything is not right, they will be the first to report it. You should also consider giving them some latitude and trust, which will allow them to grow.

Summary

In this chapter, I have outlined some basic principles of cybersecurity:

- Change requires putting humans at the centre.

  - You do not need to lead the change alone.

  - Use the power of champions.

- In order for your company to adopt a *culture of cybersecurity*, you must be the epicentre.

- Education is an inspiration game. No one will take this seriously if you, as a leader, don't.

- Your executive team will need to be inspired into action.

- Cybersecurity is based on data, which creates clarity.

- Security is an ecosystem – all parts must be aware of all other parts.

- Just like fire drills, practice makes perfect.

Now that you have educated yourself, on-boarded your management team and empowered your staff, you are ready to construct your cyberdefences.

FOUR

Construct

The third stage in the SECURE method involves constructing a customized security strategy based on the findings of your initial survey. This might include adopting stronger network security measures, improving data encryption, using more secure authentication methods or implementing a more robust intrusion detection system.

Before you start

One thing that you will need to keep in mind when constructing your security environment is that simplicity trumps complexity. That may sound counter-intuitive but bear with me for a second. The more technology you add, the more complex it becomes to monitor, and the less expertise you will have in each technology type.

Furthermore, the various technologies on the market have distinct origins. They have been grown in different labs. Compatibility and standards, especially in the cybersecurity space, will vary greatly.

Last but not least, with the current talent shortage, no one can afford to have a team of fifty people managing the systems for a company of 200.

When constructing your strategy, always remember the principle that *less is more*: you want it to be as concise and focused as possible.

Draw a plan

You need to begin by going back to your survey, where you identified what you most need to protect. To return to the building analogy I have used in previous chapters, before you go shopping for an alarm system, you need to know how many rooms, doors and windows the property has. In the same way, you should draw a plan of your company that shows each of its separate buildings, departments and offices.

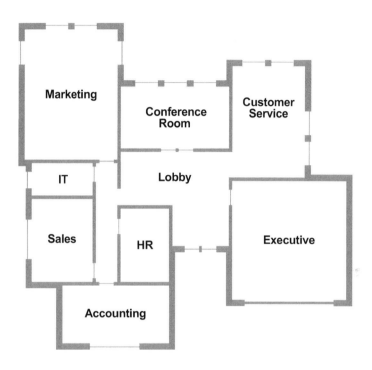

As part of your plan, you will need to define your structure so that you can, for example, create multiple networks to segment different floors or departments, or create a section of the network to publish services to the internet.

Remember our reference to medieval castle architecture, with layers upon layers of protection? This concept, known as enclaves, should be used to add layers of protection for critical services and data. Such a structure might look like this.

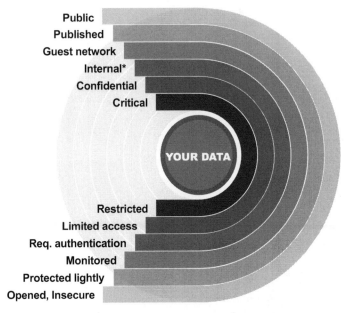

Public
Published
Guest network
Internal*
Confidential
Critical

YOUR DATA

Restricted
Limited access
Req. authentication
Monitored
Protected lightly
Opened, Insecure

*including remote users
and remote sites

The idea is to make sure your most precious treasure does not sit next to a window.

Get ready to receive logs: Create an alarm central

In order to know what is going on in each 'room', you will need to have eyes everywhere. In other words, the logs and audits will need to be assembled somewhere – the equivalent of a central alarm console. Before you start deploying 'sensors' and 'smoke detectors', you must therefore create a place to send all this data.

Where to send the signals: The SIEM

The SIEM (*Security Information and Event Management*) is used to collect and correlate all security signals that will be collected by your various sensors.

Consider the following, each device within your environment is emitting, every second, information about what is happening. That data must be collected and, more importantly, correlated with all devices around it.

It will also allow the enrichment of the base signals with threat intelligence, which will automatically recognize certain patterns or behaviours. As an example, in its cloud environment, Microsoft receives 64 trillion signals per day, which are analysed through machine-learning algorithms, allowing their customers to share this intelligence. When a cybercriminal tries using a particular malware on your environment, it may be the 100th time Microsoft has seen it. Threat recognized, instantly.

Your SIEM deployment will evolve as your environment evolves. For example, say in six months you choose to change a system, for example, a firewall, your SIEM will need to be configured to receive signals from this new partner.

In my Microsoft world, I would use Microsoft Sentinel, which would provide not only storage for all audits and logs, but also a pre-emptive, automated reaction when known threats are detected.

What to do with the alerts: The SOAR

The SOAR (*Security Orchestration Automation and Response*) is your automated helper. It will allow you to create automated reactions: for example, if an attack of type X is detected, here is the series of actions to be performed. The idea is to isolate the machine, for example, before the malware spreads to other computers within your environment.

The only challenge with a SOAR environment is that it is not magic. It does not learn on its own or automate the reaction by itself. Someone has to build the automation playbooks and test and tweak them.

The beauty of this, though, is that those functionalities are often built into SOAR systems, and within Microsoft Sentinel, for example, there is a worldwide community that contributes to automation rules and playbooks. This is also true for complex queries and finding information on a given subject in your environment. Often, the community will have shared examples and queries that will support your team.

You are not alone.

How to make sense through the noise: The alert plan

The first few months after setting up the alarm centre will be hectic. You have to be wary of alert fatigue, which can occur when there are so many alerts that you eventually don't even want to look at them.

This means that you need to invest the first few months tweaking the alerts to ensure that you only receive what is urgent and that most of the annoyances are taking care of themselves.

The beauty of it is that there is a dial for just about everything. All alert sources can be tweaked to be more (or less) informative.

The alert plan will not reduce the quantity of information available to dig through in the event of an incident, it just reduces the number of times your monitoring teams' phone buzzes during the night.

More importantly, it reduces the number of false positives.

Strengthen your identity

As we know, the thing that cybercriminals want more than anything else is your identity. If they can act on your behalf, they can do whatever you can: access your bank accounts, transfer money, sell your house…

Furthermore, if your credentials (usernames, passwords) carry any elevated privileges, they can alter your company's systems and services and infest everything in them.

By this point, you have a complete overview of the various processes and technologies you can put in place to protect your users' and services' identities. To strengthen your identity, you should do the following:

Use multifactor authentication (MFA)

Using MFA is like adding a third lock to your door. Your username and password are strengthened by the fact that the system will also ask for another, unique key, such as a code or a number from your personal smartphone.

Have different passwords for different services

If you remember my 'one password for all' horror story, you will understand the importance of this. Over the past twenty years, processing power has increased exponentially. A mobile phone today is at least twenty times more powerful than an early PC. As technology advances still further, it will take less and less time for cybercriminals to 'crack' passwords using what is known as 'brute force'. A password that might have taken them a week to work out twenty years ago can now be broken in less than two hours.

As we have also seen, it is now possible for a criminal to 'steal' your password by listening to your keyboard as you type it – a process known as keylogging.

Enable single sign-on (SSO)

If possible, reduce the number of users/passwords to enable a single sign-on, meaning that with a single identity, users can access all their required services.

This will make it possible for people to have a single identity, which can be used to access numerous services. It is a double-edged sword, however – easier to use and maintain, but giving access to more services. It will need to be highly secured. EntraID can be that service for multiple cloud-provided services.

One example of this is to integrate your corporate PC with your Microsoft 365 identity. When you then log in to the Office 365 portal or Microsoft 365 apps, your identity will automatically be known and there is no need for relogging.

Use a password vault

To overcome these problems, I recommend using a password vault (see Chapter 3). A good password vault should have:

- A master password, ideally one that supports a second factor beyond the password (MFA), which is the code to your vault, the one password that allows access to it

- A zero-trust architecture, which means that the manufacturer of the vault will not have access to your passwords

- The capacity to autogenerate new passwords

- The capacity to autofill requests for known usernames and passwords

- The capacity to create an identity card (username, password and MFA) and to share it with members of a team without divulging the password

- The capacity to host credit card information and to autofill credit card requests

- The capacity for cross-platform password management, eg Windows, Mac, iOS and Android

Use biometrics or a passwordless model

All new devices now have built-in biometrics, which means that you can use a part of your body – your face or your fingerprint, for example – as your 'password'. Alternatively, you can use a mobile device or a plug-in token as identification. Some tokens ask for your fingerprint once you have plugged them in, providing an extra layer of authentication.

Such technology will ultimately enable you to adopt a passwordless model.

Enable identity protection

The last step towards protecting your identity is to protect your source of truth, which is the platform that you are using for everyone in your company to rely on. In Microsoft 365, that would be EntraID, and if you have an on-premises network, it is most likely Active Directory.

Beyond basic operational hygiene (meaning that accounts are disabled and then archived when an employee leaves), there are services that can be put in place to help you see hidden patterns in user behaviour, the ones only revealed by behaviour analytics.

Here are some questions to ask yourself:

- How will my identity providers be protected?
  - Services such as Defender for Identity and Identity Protection can serve this role for Microsoft 365 users.
- How will I ensure that my service identity remains confidential?

- Will my users require multifactor authentication?

- What countries will I block from authenticating to your environment? For example, do I need people from China, Iran or North Korea logging in or do I seek to exclude them?

- How will I manage passwords?

  - Am I going to establish a centralized password vault?

  - Am I going to go passwordless?

  - Am I going to ask users to have complex passwords?

Here are the points that you want your solution to respond to:

- Privileged access management

- Risky sign-in analysis and reports

- Behavioural analysis

- Inactivity reporting, which flags accounts that have not signed in in the last three or six months – such accounts should usually be disabled

- Lateral movement/escalation alerts

- Integration into your alarm centre

This will provide you with visibility into your identity provider.

Best practice dictates that you should, as far as possible, synchronize your internal directory and your cloud service provider, as this will greatly simplify your and your users' lives. By synchronizing identities, you will be able to achieve single sign-on (see above).

Finally, you must 'sell' your plan to your users to ensure that they are properly educated and on-boarded. Yes, this will slightly complicate their lives, but once the process is embedded in their way of working, they will hardly even notice it.

Strengthening your identity using these tools may not prevent or repel a cyberattack, but it will buy you the most valuable commodity: time. With that time, you will be able to react, change a password, close access to an intruder that comes from abroad, or put in place extra security to quarantine the bad actor.

Build your security system

Now that you have drawn a plan of your company, created an alarm centre and put in place adequate identity protection, you are in a position to secure your systems and deploy your alarm sensors, the aim of which is to spot attack attempts when they come in, see what they are trying to do and stop them before they do any serious damage.

Perimeter and networks

We have discussed the importance – and limitations – of firewalls, which guard the door and fence off your network. The reason for deploying sensors here is to tell your alarm centre every time someone starts knocking on the door, as well as alert it if any devices within your network try to exfiltrate data in large quantities or connect to the dark web.

Devices

As we have seen, nine times out of ten, devices are the 'conduit' through which identities are broken, malware infects the system and data gets exfiltrated. When a cybercriminal gets their hands on a powerful device, running on a privileged identity, they can rapidly spread infection throughout your company. If they do, you therefore want to know about it immediately.

In order to know what is happening on your devices, you will want them to be managed, so you will be able to have some telemetry, to know if they are compliant with your rules.

The beauty of it is that most people using Microsoft 365 have access to Intune. This MDM (Managed

Devices Management) tool is used for three specific functions:

- Deploy applications (such as an EDR)
- Keep Windows devices up to date
- Configure security policies

That is the reason I use the analogy of deploying smoke detectors onto devices. They are the *endpoints* to your network – where the nerves terminate. This is the place where you want to deploy sensors. If it rings, you know something is happening, and it will act as your early warning.

The challenge with devices nowadays is not only that they carry a lot more data than they used to, but also that they move around. Mobility means that they are likely to access multiple networks and are more likely to be stolen. So you will need to decide what (type of) devices you will host on your various networks and how they will behave when they are outside the perimeter to ensure that, wherever they are and no matter what platform they are used on, your data will be secure.

You want to make sure that, if a device is accessing your data or your services, you are managing at least some of its settings – ie those that affect your company. You don't need (or want) access to personal data or services.

Especially for desktops and laptops, you want to ensure that their hard disks are encrypted so that, if they are stolen, the data held on them will be protected. Depending on the software used, there can be a performance impact, but on Windows, for example, BitLocker can be used to encrypt your hard disk and USB storage without much impact – and the functionality is built-in.

As mentioned earlier, it is important to set up EDR on your devices so that you will be alerted if anything fishy happens, and you will want it to be attached to the alarm centre to make sure that it is constantly monitored.

Hardware and, especially, operating system manufacturers such as Microsoft, are constantly publishing updates containing not only functional fixes but also security and weakness fixes. It is important to ensure that they are promptly installed (another thing to educate your staff about).

If you use Microsoft 365, the simplest way to ensure that all your devices are encrypted, that updates are promptly deployed, that you have the same base software deployed everywhere and so on, is to use Intune, a product included in its E3 and Business Premium packages.

Applications

The next thing to check is that you have an application inventory and that it is up to date, and that you are in a position to know if the applications you are using to access and manage your sensitive data have security weaknesses. Are they, for example, being tested for security by their manufacturers?

The easiest way to do this is to keep a minimal inventory – an application portfolio that you need for your company to operate – which you maintain religiously. From there, you should ensure that you have a matrix of all users and ensure that this too is kept up to date. Finally, check that all fixes and security patches are deployed, ensuring that you minimize what is known as your 'attack surface'.

Note that, if you have had any custom applications created, it is your responsibility to keep them up to date and to ensure that the data hosted within these applications is secured.

Data

The first thing you must ensure is that all devices that are accessing your data are protected and monitored. This means that, at any time, you can tell who is accessing what. You can also tell if someone is attempting to access something that is protected.

This might seem rather 'Big Brotherly' but, when I work with CEOs, I always ask them these two simple questions: 'What would be the cost to your company if your data is compromised? Can you afford the reputational impact of having all your corporate secrets exposed?' Invariably, they cannot immediately answer the first question, but their answer to the second question is invariably, 'No'.

We have talked about different types of data and levels of access to it, and about encryption and tagging, which will help you to create an inventory. Now you must decide how much security to impose on what data. If you tighten it too much, your staff will no longer be able to work; leave it too loose and it might 'disappear'.

As is so often the case, it is a 'balancing act', but even if you decide to err on the side of looseness, the occasional message saying something like, 'Excuse me, do you realize that you are about to send confidential information outside the organization' would not go amiss.

Servers and services

Servers and services are the holy grail for cybercriminals, who will usually try to infiltrate them through your devices. Whether physical or virtual, these therefore need to be protected and monitored, so that if there is unusual activity or behaviour or an inbound attack, your response team will be aware and able to react. An inbound attack means, for example, that a port has been left exposed to the internet and that a weakness has been used to get in.

We have seen that your business relies on a variety of services, some of which have inherent weaknesses just asking to be exploited. The solution is to make a checklist and ensure that you have a palliative measure in place for each one. For example, in Microsoft 365, you can force it to use modern authentication and deprecate its former authentication method.

Here are some things to check:

- That the data is hosted in-country; if not, obtain documented approval from management that this data is not sensitive or critical before hosting it outside the company's country of residence. If the data is under a third party's responsibility, ensure that the service agreements are reviewed by legal experts.

- That access to each service is protected by modern authentication, preferably integrated with your main corporate identity through SSO.

- That client-server communication is protected through a security certificate. This means that the data is encrypted, and hence, if captured, it would be useless.

- That each service is given a sensitivity and criticality 'score' so that you know its recovery priority should a problem occur.

- How is data backed up and whether it will remain available should there be an issue.

- How the data is protected against extraction – eg through encryption at rest and in transit.*

- That, depending on its sensitivity, a monthly or yearly review of the security of your data is made by your provider (which might be required by their certification status, such as ISO 27001).

Depending on the service criticality, you may need to establish a service-level agreement. This means that, if the service is not available for a period, the service provider must pay a penalty.

- **Remote users, local networks:** If your users are working remotely and you are hosting your own services, you will need to define how they will access these services. The usual way is through a virtual private network (VPN). This allows users to access your network through an encrypted tunnel. The main issue with this model is that you need to trust the device at the other end, which requires very tight control, as you are exposing your network to an outside source.

---

* *At rest*: meaning while being stored, unused. *In transit*: meaning while transiting between the service and the end user's device.

- **Remote users, remote services:** This is where cloud services make the most sense. No matter where your users are, your services are published globally. You have a single set of services to secure, and your users can access them from wherever they are. Instead of creating an encryption tunnel, services are published through an encrypted protocol, SSL, hence setting up expensive VPNs isn't required.

- **Remote users, hybrid services:** If you have separate offices or manufacturing sites, you can create what are known as site-to-site VPNs, allowing you to stretch the perimeter of these sites to the cloud, which in effect becomes your own private data centre.

Messaging

We have seen that messaging is possibly the 'weakest link' in your defences against cyberattacks. Here are a few things that can help you to secure your email systems:

- MAPI protocol introduction (replacing SMTP, POP3 and IMAP in Microsoft Exchange servers and Microsoft 365)

- DNS entries that provide spam handling (DMARC, SPIF)

- Domain encryption keys (DKIM)

- Email encryption (S/Mime)

- Threat protection rules against spam, malware and impersonation

- SafeLinks and SafeAttachment*

The threat protection rules you deploy are learning rules, meaning they are powered by machine learning. These rules are integrated into threat intelligence feeds that are aware of the various spam and phishing campaigns worldwide and even learn from the spam being tagged at your organization. This greatly reduces the risk of malware entering your environment.

The main drawback to all this protection is false positives – genuine emails that get put into quarantine. This aspect of your cybersecurity strategy may require a little 'hand-holding' until your staff learns to manage their quarantine, but there is light at the end of that tunnel: as cloud providers' machine-learning algorithms become smarter, the number of false positives will likely diminish over time.

Enable auditing

When I started in technology, some years ago, system administrators were often reluctant to set up auditing

---

* Part of Microsoft Defender for 365, these allow links and attachments to be pre-opened in the cloud and tested for toxicity before allowing them to be opened on the end user's device.

logs on servers due to their impact on processing speed and disk space. This is no longer a concern.

Now cybercriminals make these logs essential because if you don't have them, you will never know if someone leaves with your data, if a system is attacked or if you are robbed. Audits are your security cameras, and yes, you want them recording all the time.

Auditing has to be set up at every level so that you have traceability. Here are some examples:

- All file accesses
- Authentication attempts (both failed and successful), including:
  - Time
  - Location
- File transfers in/out of:
  - Your device
  - Your network
  - Your servers/services
- Messaging in/out
- Script/program execution – for example, if someone launches a script on a workstation that tries to steal data or makes a malicious call

You may think this is an awful lot of information to collect, but without it, you will rapidly lose all trace of any data that goes astray or is lost. With it, you have a fighting chance of tracing it back and reporting the attack to the authorities so that they can intervene.

With minimal blind spots, you will be able to play back the crime scene and might even be able to roll back some of its consequences.

Set up a monitoring service

If you deploy all this wonderful tech, train your people and change your processes but don't monitor anything that is happening, the cybercriminals will still win. Yes, you will have complicated their lives, but they won't give up that easily. Someone knowledgeable must be looking at what is happening and be ready to react – at all times.

So the monitoring service is the manning of your alarm centre. Who are going to be the analysts looking at all these logs?

You may not feel that you need a 24/7 monitoring service, but how likely is it that an attack will take place between 9am and 5pm, Monday to Friday? Do you really think that cybercriminals will do you the favour of attacking you during normal business hours?

The good news is that you can outsource that service for a fraction of the price of hiring a team of cybersecurity analysts.

Keep registries, logs and controls

Registries will need to be maintained to ensure that your team knows what is happening and what should happen when an event occurs. Also, if you need to reconstruct the timeline of an incident, which you almost certainly will, it is crucial to know where and when things happened.

Here is an example (a true story).

RETRACING THE PAYLOAD

We were called in to recover an engineering firm (thirty engineers) in Montreal after a cyberattack they had had a month previously. One of the engineers had received an email with a malware attachment. He had opened it as it was from a known recipient.

His computer started misbehaving afterwards but when the on-site technician ran their existing antivirus he found nothing, so the computer was considered clean.

Thirty days later, the entire company went down.

Because there was no registry tracking the events leading up to the crash, we had to interview five people and dig through thousands of emails before we finally traced the original payload. This took two of us almost a whole day – an eternity in terms of incident response.

The direct impact of not having a registry was a delayed recovery effort. A day might not seem much, but when you consider that no one could work and the time spent digging and not recovering, we were rapidly getting near the $100,000 mark. To say nothing of the potential impact to the company's reputation.

The registry without auditing and monitoring logs would still have made this research impossible.

This is where the need for controls comes in. You need to implement a routine whereby both the registry and the logs are controlled. The registry has to be validated as being properly filled in with the right information and logs properly collected. If that is not the case, this needs to be rectified. Controls encourage discipline.

Problem solving

As you build this system of security, you will discover blind spots: a lot of unforeseen problems and challenges will show up. This is normal. It will, however, require agility on your part, as well as a healthy dose of patience. Your cybersecurity strategy will need to be what we call a 'living document', meaning that it will need to evolve and be revised regularly.

Risks will show up after an audit, after finding a breach or after being attacked, whether successful or not. There are only two ways to address a newfound risk: either you accept it and live with it, or you implement a fix. Whichever you choose, you will need to keep a registry in which all new risks are noted. Accepted risks are a liability to the company, therefore an executive must sign and approve it.

My Cyber Plan

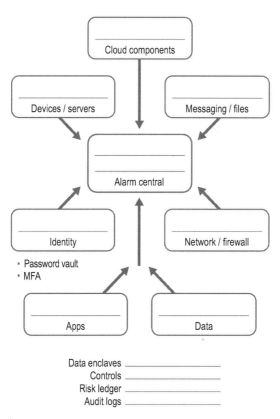

Your risk registry must be reviewed at regular intervals, especially if an event alters your environment, whether a merger, a new technology or a change in your ecosystem (such as the COVID pandemic, which led to a sudden increase in remote working).

Once you have constructed your cybersecurity system, it is essential to ensure that it remains 'alive'. We will be discussing how to do this in the final chapter of the book.

Summary

The Construct phase of the SECURE model begins with a plan of your security structure, protecting what is most important and valuable to your company. You must then create an alarm centre to monitor your security 24/7.

Before actually building your security system, you must strengthen your identity and that of your users. Auditing the system is a must, as are the teams that will monitor your alarm centre 24/7. Regular updates of registries and logs, including a registry of all new risks that arise, are also essential.

Here are the key takeaways from this chapter:

- Your strategy must be customized to your terrain.

- Less is more.

- Your people must be involved at every stage.

- Structure and discipline make things simpler.

Construction involves bringing together a lot of technologies and building multiple layers of protection. In the next phase, Unify, your goal will be to bring together the people using your processes and technology in order to turn your strategy into a culture.

FIVE
Unify

As I have said before, cybersecurity isn't just about technology; it is also about processes and people. In this chapter, you will learn the importance of creating unified security protocols across all departments and ensuring alignment between IT and other business functions. This consistency will help prevent security gaps and confusion, improving your company's overall security.

In addition, I will discuss the extension of your strategy to your 'ecosystem' – the companies (clients, suppliers, providers, subcontractors) that you do business with, which also need to be secure to maintain your own security.

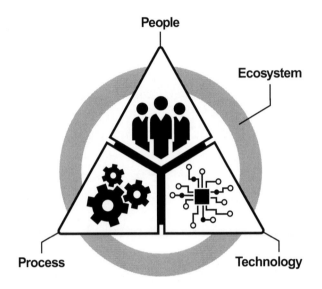

Here are a few examples of how these four 'pillars' must work together:

- You can have the best network protection in the world, but if your receptionist mistakes a stranger for one of your new technicians and grants them access to a closed office, that protection will be useless.

- You can have perfectly trained employees, but if your process sends your contracts for treatment to a third party who transfers them to an unprotected site, in an unregulated country, that training will be wasted.

- You can have great staff and perfectly tuned processes, but if you put your data in unprotected storage or leave it on a publicly accessible computer, you might as well not have bothered.

- Then there is this last, the newcomer to the party: you can have done everything right, open your network to a new supplier who is not secured, and boom! Your data is leaving the building.

The key thing to remember is that, if you, as a business leader, do not believe cybersecurity to be important, that will have a ripple effect through your entire company – though the very fact that you are reading this book reassures me that this is not the case.

People

Creating a 'culture of cybersecurity' means making cybersecurity just as much a part of life in your company as regulating the air-conditioning or refilling the coffee machine – something that hardly even needs conscious thought. It also means that everyone feels responsible for keeping your company and its data secure and accountable for any failure to do so. Essentially, it is a question of awareness.

Always keep in mind that cybersecurity is a balancing act between freedom and security. Whatever you gain in security, you lose in freedom, in privacy. Someone will know what you are doing. You will no longer be free to do whatever you want.

If you have ever wondered why CISOs (Chief Information Security Officers) don't usually last long (their average 'lifetime' in a company is two years), it is because, being responsible for cybersecurity, they are stuck between a rock and a hard place. Their job, by definition, makes them 'the enemy of the people'. They have to create and enforce policies and, most of the time, they don't have sufficient budgets to train people, manage change or even tell people why their freedom is being restricted. This means that, not only are they generally regarded as a nuisance (or an unnecessary expense), but their underfunded and underappreciated efforts often leave holes that criminals can exploit. So one of three things usually happens: they leave, they burn out, or there is a cyber-security incident.

Accountability

All your employees must understand the serious-ness of cybersecurity. As a friend of mine, who hap-pens to be the CEO of a large accounting firm, put it: cybersecurity is a team sport; the whole team has to be responsible for whether we win or lose.

As in any sport, rules must be set and understood. As Simon Sinek puts it in his well-known book, this is an 'infinite game',[17] in which there are no winners or los-ers, but you are playing against yourself in a bid to get better and better, day after day.

Of course, in this game, everyone has a lot to lose. Customers' data can be compromised, the company can be sued, intellectual property can be stolen... There is a lot at stake, so it needs to be taken seriously.

No one in your company must be left out of cybersecurity. If a person does not comply, they become your weakest link. In one company I worked for, we used to change the background images on all the computers that were left unlocked at the end of the day or for any prolonged period during it. It was a childish prank, but it sent out an important message: if you leave your device unlocked and without surveillance, anyone can do things on your behalf. People soon locked their computers whenever they were away from their desks.

Having a culture of cybersecurity will ensure that your receptionist will ask the right questions and log the appropriate information before letting anyone into the building, that your office staff will think twice before clicking on any link within an email, and that your assistant will check and double-check – and obtain the necessary authority – before transferring any funds during a merger or acquisition.

If something unusual happens or there is an unexpected error, the alarm must be raised automatically and immediately, just as it would be if a fire broke out.

Consider this example: a company president calls me one morning and says, 'René-Sylvain, something's wrong. I've just had to reauthenticate my OneDrive five times.' After checking that nothing is wrong with his device, I start looking into his credentials. A bit of digging in the sign-in logs of the Entra ID[18] soon reveals that he has been the victim of a password spray attack (see Chapter 3).

This is the type of reflex your team and your operations must develop, as opposed to thinking nothing of having to enter their password ten times or being asked to change it because 'it isn't secure'. It will take time, but it is worth the effort.

Agreements and policies

To make sure that everyone is taking responsibility for their actions, it is helpful to draw up agreements and implement policies. Having to sign something that says you are aware of your cybersecurity responsibilities makes it real. Policies will also create boundaries so that your employees know what is the sandbox in which they are allowed (or not allowed) to play.

Here are some policies that you may want to define:

- Terms of engagement (how will technology be used at your company)

- Digital hygiene (how to clean your online data)

- Netiquette (proper use, language and behaviour online)

- Privacy and confidentiality

- Customers' data

- Corporate intellectual property

These documents, once signed and accepted by everyone in your community, will provide a framework within which they work and, in the event of a cyber-incident, will prevent cybercriminals from publishing information about employees who are using their corporate emails and computers for personal and potentially reputation-damaging purposes such as accessing pornography or dubious 'dating' sites.

Standard agreements and policies should be part of your employee onboarding process so that they know from the word go that they are responsible and accountable for their actions with regards to cybersecurity.

Having such policies and agreements will also help you to comply with laws and regulations that you are required to abide by, since you will already be doing most of what you need to do, such as:

- Documenting your processes

- Creating an enclave for your compliance data

- Tagging your compliance-related data

- Maintaining a registry

- Establishing controls

Once you have established your strategy and procedures, integrating certification and compliance is simply about adapting the terms and conditions you are already using.

Technology

Understanding that you have constructed your new cyberdefences in the Construct phase, you must now ensure that your technology layer is integrated with your updated security standards.

The following sections provide guidelines for unifying cybersecurity with your other technologies.

Zero trust

In zero-trust architecture, nothing is taken for granted. It is like having a security guard at every door in your business, checking IDs and making sure that only authorized personnel are allowed in. This means, for example, that it is not because a user identifies himself as 'John324' that he will automatically be trusted, or that because an order comes from the email or the phone of the president it will automatically be honoured.

The same goes for devices. Nowadays, even a machine within a local network behind a firewall can no longer be trusted. It can be compromised.

The main principles of a zero-trust architecture are:

- **Always verify:** Always authenticate and authorize using all available data points – user identity, location, device, service, etc. Incorporate behavioural data and get context from the entire IT stack (identity, endpoint, workload, etc). Always make sure that a person is who they say they are, and that a machine meets all compliance requirements – on every access.

- **Always assume breaches:** Whenever someone tries to access data, assume that a machine has been breached and be on your guard. This is more of a mindset to adopt as part of the company culture than a technical implementation. It is better to block and then ask than to be compromised.

- **Always monitor:** Constantly be aware of what is happening and keep track of everything, so that you can reconstruct the complete story if necessary. This principle is covered in detail in Chapter 5.

- **Use least privileges:** Accord everyone the minimum level of privileges necessary for them to do their work – also known as privileged access management (PAM) or just-in-time (JIT) and just-enough access (JEA). In other words, avoid giving god-like powers to anyone and make sure there is an automated way to revoke those privileges once the agreed time expires.

Let's look at how you might put two of these principles into practice – always verify and use least privileges.

Always verify

In layman's terms, don't trust anything you are told. You need to verify that the computer authenticating to gain access to your system is truly the device that it says it is.

This allows the detection of attacks like 'impossible travel', which means that a first authentication comes from Montreal and a few moments later, one comes from Tokyo. This is where the attack's name comes from – the user or device could not have travelled so far, so fast, hence, someone is trying to impersonate it (trying to pass for someone else). The advantage of making devices part of the authentication chain is that they follow their users everywhere. If, for example, a computer suddenly authenticates in Toronto instead of Montreal, but your authenticator is also in Toronto, then the system can safely assume that you are in Toronto. You can neutralize threats such as impersonation by collecting metrics such as behaviour and location.

This is where MFA becomes key. It forces any user accessing your corporate data not only to show that they know the required username and password for the device or system they are accessing, but also to present an SMS or verification via Microsoft's Authenticator app, for example, to confirm their identity. It's like having the alarm's code when walking into the house. You have the address and the key, but you also have something that only you can know, the code.

It is both harder and simpler for service accounts. Service accounts are generic accounts that you create to do a specific or repeatable task, to act as a system administrator. Scripts are pieces of code that are necessary to automate jobs to help the environment run smoothly. Service accounts are used so that those scripts can be executed with elevated privileges. The issue is that there is no way to prove that the script is truly doing what it is supposed to do and that it has not been tampered with. But the good news is that scripts are highly predictable, in their duration, the intervals at which they run and so on. Behavioural data becomes key.

The key to this is committing to your identity source. In most cases, Entra ID will be your trusted cloud identity provider, while most of the planet also runs Active Directory internally.

Use least privileges

Consider for a moment that your team of twenty system administrators and technicians all have complete control over your environment. If any one of them has their credentials compromised, you have suddenly lost control of your *entire* environment.

With privileged access management, each user has to request (and justify) the need for heightened privilege for a specific duration. Suddenly, only one person is your global administrator, so you have reduced your potential attack surface by 95%.

Furthermore, any heightened privileges within your environment are now audited and a registry exists with all the reasons why that right was given to that person for that amount of time. Then, if a breach does occur, it is nineteen times easier for you to trace its cause – which also means that it is nineteen times more likely that the person responsible will do their work diligently and responsibly.

Getting your staff on board with this one can be a delicate operation since you are asking some of your key users to let go of their privileges. It is a matter of education: of making them understand that the goal is to reduce (dramatically) your attack surface.

This might all sound somewhat paranoid, and when you look at your processes through the lens of zero trust, you will start putting little red flags at various checkpoints. But try not to be overwhelmed by the number of red flags; tackle them one at a time. Have someone survey your key information and processes and identify the weaknesses in them. You might consider some to be acceptable risks (but make sure they are entered in your risk registry along with who accepted them and when), while others will need to be addressed as a priority.

Training and testing

To obtain some contracts – particularly with any branch of government – you will be required to train your employees in cybersecurity, as well as such subjects as ethics and governance. Regular training sessions on the latest threats, safe practices and company security policies should in any case be part of your overall cybersecurity strategy.

Cybersecurity companies will offer a service known as *spear phishing*. This, coupled with training, is the best combination. Spear phishing is a form of targeted phishing that uses emails aimed at testing your employees' awareness. The idea is for your management or IT team to launch false attacks on your unsuspecting staff, so that you can identify who needs to be further trained on the various aspects of cybersecurity.

You probably have regular fire drills in your company just as you did at school (if you can remember that far back). Everyone knows exactly what to do and where to meet and it all runs like clockwork, without people even having to think about it. This choreography is the result of years of practice. This is why you need regular 'cyber drills'.

I strongly recommend that, as soon as your action plan is built, you practise it at least once a quarter, until it is a natural reflex for your entire management team and staff: everyone is ready at all times and knows exactly what they have to do. It can also help, if you can afford it, to be supported by professionals, such as cyberse-curity firms, to validate your plan, and also have a list of experts that you will require in case of a real cyber-attack, lawyers, a PR firm, IT professionals, and so on.

Keeping the plan up to date

As I have said (several times) before, it is essential to keep your cybersecurity strategy up to date. The methods of cybercriminals are becoming ever-more devious and the technology available to them ever-more sophisticated, and you must always be one step ahead of them.

The following (true) story, though not a cybersecurity incident, illustrates the point clearly.

THE OLD AND THE NEW

In July 2012, a significant incident occurred at a data centre in Calgary, Canada, which had a profound impact on key services both in the city and throughout the province of Alberta.

An explosion, followed by a fire, resulted in the data centre being flooded by the building's sprinkler systems. This resulted in numerous systems, both primary and backup, being incapacitated. Among these was the system that governed the province's health service.

Fortunately, with the help of a multinational firm, the directors had created a recovery plan and had been practising it regularly since 1998. Within a week, the centre's essential systems were back online – all except the email system.

Unfortunately, as an enquiry to their service provider revealed, email had not been prioritized and so was not due to come back online for another three weeks.

The fact was that, in 1998, email was just an accessory, a toy, not considered vital to operations. By 2012, the year of the incident, it had become integrated into most processes, which could not function properly without it but the fourteen-year-old plan, which had been learned to the letter, had never been updated.

Within a week, the board voted to move all messaging to Office 365, and the email system was back up and running.

We will be looking at this issue in greater depth in Chapter 7.

Processes

As we know, the primary goal of a cybercriminal is to gain access to your company's data. To do this, they will mine your credentials until they get the access they need; to do that, they will create multiple personas, disguises to make themselves look like any normal resident of your environment. What could be more normal than a process? If they can infiltrate a few processes and modify them slightly, not only can they get a sense of what is happening within your company, but also they will have a vehicle that will run regularly, under the radar and without any need for them to expose themselves.

Let's explore that a little more. Say you have a process that runs payroll. A normal process that runs every second week. What if, within that process, a line of code is added that sends the payroll file to a dark web address, and a second line further down ensures that malware is downloaded to your file server and schedules a job to reinitiate the malware if it has been disabled? Suddenly, within your payroll system, you are exporting your corporate private information and reinitializing a threat, all under the radar as the payroll is just a normal process.

If your data is the information that runs your business, your processes are its nervous system, which is necessary to carry that information throughout the company. But unlike your nervous system, this network of automated actions is usually owned by multiple humans, which makes them hard to map. Just like your nervous system, it can be fooled, perhaps even hacked.

That is why they need to be unified in your security model.

Remember when I said earlier that service accounts were both the best and worst thing? Well, here's a perfect example: what if an automated process requires access rights to a system, but those credentials are unencrypted and sit in a text file? You have a potential breach, and not only are those credentials just sitting there ready to be (ab)used, but also – and worse – you don't know it. You won't know it until they are used against you.

Although it was not written by him, Peter Ducker is often credited with saying 'you can't improve what you don't measure'. The corollary of this is: what is measured improves. If there is one lesson I have learned from my years within large corporations it is this: if you don't pay any attention to the security of your processes, they will never get any better.

Imagine that you have a simple process that is responsible for automatically taking data from your HR system and sending it to your payroll department. Your employees have made sure that the data in both systems is encrypted, in case it gets stolen. This is a simple process. A script will be used to do the work. The script contains the credentials that have access to both systems. If this script is not stored carefully, those credentials are exposed (remember earlier, clear text). What does that mean? It means that, over time, if a bad actor gets access to this file, he gets the credentials, which means that he has read access to all your employees' HR information and write access into your payroll system. Basically, the credentials are the key to decrypting the data.

Worse, those credentials can now be used to attempt escalation to other systems. It is like finding a key in an apartment building. Does it open only one door or is it a master key? As a weakness rarely comes alone, the same username and password might have been reused in other places or could have enough privileges to give itself more access.

By itself it may not look like this would derail the company, but if you take it to the extreme, how much disruption can be created when someone has the ability to resell personal identifiable information (PII) and can disrupt all your employee's payroll? The answer is quite a bit.

Securing processes to ensure survivability

If your processes are the nervous system of your company, what happens if any of them is compromised or deleted? The company stops. Securing your processes will ensure survivability.

As I just demonstrated, the *identity* portion is important when it comes to process automation. It is one of many pieces that you need to be thinking about when inspecting processes. Here are a few to get you thinking:

- Identity: How you authenticate against each system. Least privilege is favoured here.

- Encryption: Not only of the data but also, as we have seen, of any scripts and documentation.

- Storage: The location where you store results, processes and various automation scripts must also be protected.

- Traceability and auditing: Are you able to trace what was done, when, and by whom?

- Having a way to recreate if lost: A securely stored, restorable copy of the process so that, if lost, it does not have to be rebuilt from scratch.

- Monitoring: If you have processes that are critical to your business, monitoring their behaviour is probably a good idea.

And I am not kidding anyone. This takes work and it will not come cheap.

Ecosystem

The standard motto for cybersecurity has always been 'people, processes and technology'. But recent supply chain attacks have shown that the ecosystem is now so tightly integrated that it too needs to be part of your cybersecurity discussion.

The SolarWind attack at Microsoft is one of the most publicly known examples; however, here are two of the most recent supply chain attacks:

- **Okta (2022):** A security software manufacturer was breached by the Lapsus$ group which resulted in 366 customers being impacted.[19]

- **Colonial Pipeline (2021):** Where the cybercriminals used a vulnerability in unpatched VPN software, which allowed them to remotely execute code.[20]

As soon as you open your company's network to a third party, that third party becomes a cybersecurity liability. You must therefore make sure that they are secure. If they don't handle your data as scrupulously as you do, all the work you have done will be for nothing.

If any third party needs access to your internal business data or any of your systems, you must obviously be particularly careful. Electronic Data Interchange (EDI) systems, which allow companies to exchange data faster, have been around for twenty years or more, and most are badly in need of updating to meet today's security standards. The risk is as follows: with the goal (I presume) of maximizing collaboration and flexibility, Microsoft added functionalities within Entra, their identity management solution, to establish trust between organizations. Although this is great for merger scenarios, it is also a great threat if you connect to an undisciplined, unsecured environment.

There may be value in doing this if you are about to merge two companies, but the risks, in my view, far outweigh the potential rewards. If there is any breach on either side, both companies go down.

So how *do* you unify your processes with those in your ecosystem?

Put simply, both companies have to show evidence that they are secure, and the company that has a lesser standard of cybersecurity has to rise to meet its partner – *never* the other way around. You must not at any cost lower your standards to match those of a third party. This is like telling someone you barely know that you are leaving your front door unlocked and disarming the alarm system. You might as well give them a copy of the key while you are about it.

That is why, nowadays, before giving any third party access to your data or your network, you must ask them to answer an in-depth survey regarding their cybersecurity. Such a survey should cover the following points:

- How are their devices protected?
- Are they centrally monitoring cybersecurity events?

- Have they been audited and, if so, can the results be examined?

- Have they had breaches and are they logged?

If they are truly close, you could also provide them a copy of this book, as a guide to securing their company.

Summary

In order to make both your company and your environment secure, you need to ensure that you unify people, processes, technology and your ecosystem under a common understanding. They have to act as one when responding to an incident, or even to a potential threat.

Your culture must become centred on cybersecurity, your processes must integrate best practices to ensure that your identity and your data are safe, your technology has to act as a guardrail to make sure the other three (people, processes and ecosystem) remain compliant, and your ecosystem must show their cards if they want access to your most intimate data and services.

A few things to keep in mind:

- Each of the four points has to be addressed; any weakness in any of them can create a weak point.

- People are making choices every hour of every day they work for your company. Training them will help them make the right ones, but keeping the communication lines open will allow you to know if something is wrong.

- Processes are the nervous system of your company, make sure they survive an event.

- Technology will help you delay, perhaps even stop, an incident, but it has to remain patched and up to date to ensure its reliability.

- An ecosystem is required in this digitally connected world. Make sure your partners have similar standards and are as conscientious as you are with regards to cybersecurity.

- Linking two companies may be necessary, but you need to rise to the one with the highest standards, never lower your standards.

SIX

Review

Cybercriminals never sleep and neither should your cybersecurity. We have already discussed the need for a monitoring system that will ensure that the security measures you have put in place are regularly reviewed and tested.

In this chapter, we will look at the security audits and vulnerability assessments that are necessary to identify weak points before they are exploited, as well as incident response plans and drills to ensure constant preparedness for potential security breaches.

It is a case of constantly making small, incremental changes that will improve your security over time; of training the system so that, when an incident occurs, it has acquired 'muscle memory' and knows how to respond with little of your attention being necessary.

Constant awareness

As we know, cyberattacks can come at any moment, from anywhere in the world – which means that you need to have eyes everywhere.

It is important for you to be aware of the geopolitical situation your business is in. You may not be directly implicated in an international conflict, but just being in a country that is remotely involved in such an incident can paint a target on your back.

I am not suggesting that you study every piece of news about political unrest everywhere in the world, but you should keep yourself informed about what is happening that might affect your security. Which are the most active cybercriminal groups and what is their modus operandi? What are the most virulent threats this month?

A prime example is generative AI (such as OpenAI's ChatGPT), which is increasingly affecting cybersecurity by, on the one hand, allowing criminals to create even more realistic phishing emails and new tools that can bypass known protection systems to get to their target faster and, on the other, making it easier for your teams to understand a cybersecurity event, enabling you to create smarter automated tools to carry out weakness testing, and drastically augmenting the efficiency of your monitoring system (with tools such as Microsoft Copilot for Security[21] enabling you to crawl through tons of data and find the proverbial needle in a haystack). This type of tool will also help cyber defenders to create translated and comprehensive summaries for executives without the technical slang.

The following experiment gives us a glimpse into the future power of AI-powered cyber threats.

A SNAKE CALLED BLACKMAMBA

In July 2023, in a groundbreaking experiment, researchers from HYAS used generative AI to create malware capable of bypassing EDR systems. They called it BlackMamba because it acted like the highly venomous snake of that name.

The experiment began with the AI being trained on a vast dataset of various types of malware. This training enabled the AI to understand the structure, behaviour and patterns of these malicious programs.

BlackMamba works by using a large language model (LLM) – a deep learning algorithm that can summarize and generate text at incredible speed – to create a polymorphic keylogger. This means that every time the BlackMamba malware runs, it mutates, making it able to slip, snakelike, through predictive cybersecurity software.

This future that may be all too close.[22]

You should also keep abreast of the latest developments in technology and services to help you fight cybercrime. Have any new solutions recently appeared that might be useful to you?

At the same time, it is important to be aware of what is happening with your staff. If someone is going on holiday to Columbia and needs access to their data, this should be taken into account so that they are able to do so without compromising your business. Enabling such channels reduces friction and frustration, as well as enhancing security.

Managing alerts

By now, you will have a system of 'sensors' that will alert you to anything suspicious. As mentioned, if this stores every bit of information about every activity in your company, you will get overloaded, and there is also a danger that, if you receive thousands of alerts every day, within a few weeks you no longer take them seriously. This is known as alert fatigue.

You must be smart about it. The process of thinning logs and tweaking alerts to reduce false positives and ensure that, when the alert sounds, it is for the right reason, is a necessary step. What you need is traceability. You need to be able to trace the bad actors that come in and see what they have done.

That balance will not be there from day one. It needs to be developed over time, with patience. It is more of an art than a science. The good news is that SIEM/ SOAR tools (such as Microsoft Sentinel) are getting better and better at filtering and reducing noise.

Automated response

If, like me, you are a small company, you may not have the resources to pay three teams to check on your systems around the clock. This is where an automated response system comes in.

As the name suggests, this ensures that reactions happen automatically if something seems abnormal. If the system can't clean it or resolve it, the relevant machine will be quarantined until an analyst can confirm whether the activity is normal or not.

This can be a challenge. If you have staff in multiple time zones, the team can be spread out into an operation known as 'follow the sun', which means that they each work their shifts in the daytime, wherever they are, but when you add all those shifts together, you have covered a full day. Of course, if you are all working in the same geographical region, this can be an expensive solution.

As soon as you have your monitoring and logging systems in place, you can implement Security

Information and Event Management (SIEM) or Security Orchestration, Automation, and Response (SOAR) technology, as used in a Security Operations Center (SOC). This gives your systems the capacity to automatically fight back if they identify a threat. Programs such as Microsoft Sentinel will take care of this for you.

Outsourcing

When you do things internally, your employees have your company's best interests at heart (or so you would hope), and they share your values and your corporate culture. As soon as you hand over part of your operations to a third party, that relationship changes. The operator does things their way, which may not fit your culture and objectives.

However, there are two major (potential) advantages of outsourcing your cybersecurity management: expertise and efficiency. Because all they do is manage cybersecurity, they will have expertise that you, as an engineering firm, for example, do not have, and they will do it far more efficiently than you ever could.

What you need to ensure is that they understand your business and your imperatives. Here are a few points to consider when choosing who to outsource your cybersecurity to:

- **Is cybersecurity their core business?** There are companies that offer cybersecurity as an 'add-on' service. They might be great at their core activity, but cybersecurity is too complex to be a part-time job.

- **Are they certified?** For example, do they have recognized certifications such as Microsoft, ISO or SOC2?

- **Are they verified?** Can they share the results of an audit or an external test of their effectiveness and efficiency?

- **Is their service designed for your company size?** You do not want to take on a provider that will give you low priority because they have much larger customers to focus on.

- **Are they transparent and honest?** Talk to them. If, during the conversation, they seem anything but authentic and truthful, look elsewhere.

- **Do you like their values/culture?** This is not a forced marriage; the relationship has to work smoothly. This is much more likely if you have a common culture and values.

- **Does the price make sense?** You should see savings of 20–40% in comparison with hiring an internal monitoring team. Work it out: how many people would you need to constantly monitor your cybersecurity and how much would this cost?

Above all, do not trust anyone who tells you that you will never be attacked. There is no such thing as a bulletproof solution, and risk zero is a myth. What you are looking for is advice that will strengthen your cybersecurity without jeopardizing your productivity.

Finally, I must emphasize that, if you are under attack or see anomalies in your systems or your environment that suggest an attack is imminent or impending, you should never hesitate to ask a professional for help and advice and call the authorities.

Annual audit

At least once a year, you must review how things are working. Just like a check-up with the dentist, this audit will tell you if you are on the right track. At least once a year, a third-party expert team should audit the various parts of your configuration. This will ensure that all parts of your system are configured optimally.

As with most things in life, it is just when you start thinking you are on top of your game that a curve ball comes out of left field. An annual audit will prevent you from falling into a 'comfort trap'.

Make sure, however, that what you get is what you want. I have worked for large consulting companies that produce hundreds of pages of PowerPoint reports, complete with fancy graphics, to show you how much you have drifted from your original con-figuration. That is not what you need as a small busi-ness. You need facts; you need to know where you are in terms of risk. You need to walk out with a clear list of to-dos, not fancy graphics.

If you are taking the necessary actions, this to-do list should become shorter year on year.

In order to implement the fixes, set aside a budget. These can be quite expensive or lengthy, though in some cases the cost can be minimal.

We recently carried out an audit at a game-development company. They were well structured and I was impressed by the seriousness they had applied to their cybersecurity. However, when our specialist went in, he found something that could have brought down their entire network: they had not changed their servers' backup battery (UPS) default management password. In plain English, by accessing the battery, he could have brought down entire racks of servers. Small error, major potential disruption.

Carry out simulations

What if a cyberattack occurred tomorrow? Are you ready? The only way to ensure that you are is to run simulations. Schedule a weekend with your man-agement team and your IT team and do a complete simulation. Note down everything that you are missing.

I recommend getting a coach to help you with this. It will cost you some money, but you will see a significant ROI in time saved.

After that first weekend, you will have a complete list of what is missing and what is needed. This will need to be shown to the board and/or any investors.

What then, you ask? Then you need to get into action and fix what you found. The only goal of simulations is to get better. The idea is not to burn out your executives, but to practise the muscle, so agree on a schedule – say, once a quarter – until the muscle memory kicks in, and then drop it to once every six months. Eventually, once everything is baked into your operations model, this becomes part of your yearly control review.

Intrusion testing

Once a year, you also need someone to test your defences – what is known as intrusion testing. I recommend that you hire a resource to carry out the test, without informing your staff. Let them behave normally, which will tell you a lot about the people aspect of your security as well.

Counterintuitive as it may seem, to get the most out of your testers, I recommend using several (maybe four or five) different teams on a revolving basis. I understand that once you have established a connection with a team of cybersecurity professionals and resolved any interpersonal issues that might have arisen, it becomes simple and comfortable to work with them again, but you need different viewpoints from different experts. Each one will bring their own experience, insights and, most importantly, toolkits. They will each try to access your environment in different ways. For example, one might test the default passwords on your backup system – a simple admin interface that a previous provider has overlooked.

If you do this, after the first year or so you will be able to see whether a particular provider has identified the same or more weaknesses than the team before. How deep did they go? Did they find new weaknesses you were not aware of? Are all the fixes they recommended working? And year on year, your business will improve its cyberdefences.

Testing can happen in a few ways.

External testing

This is the most brutal type of intrusion test. It comes from the outside world and will test the external walls of your castle.

Like a real cybercriminal, the tester will use every trick in the book (and quite a few that haven't been written up yet) to check whether any internet-facing doors can be opened, then try to squeeze inside. For example, they will look for an open Remote Desktop protocol, which is known to have multiple weaknesses. If so, they will sit at that door listening to all the traffic that comes through. As soon as they hear something interesting, such as a username and password, coupled with an internal IP address, they will make their move. From there, they may be able to compromise your entire network.

An external test will usually also cover your cloud services configurations. If so, you should be aware that, to run any type of intrusion testing against a cloud services provider, such as Azure, there are procedures to be followed. As a customer, you want to ensure that your provider knows that you will be running intrusion testing. They will provide you with guidelines for your testing team to follow, with a predefined schedule. Make sure that you (and your testing team) adhere to them or your company might itself be marked as a bad actor.

Internal testing

An internal test is designed to see what happens if someone is able to get into the castle. What could they gain access to from a normal user's point of view? What could be compromised if one of your devices got taken over? The user of that device does not need to have any privileges; in fact, it is better if they have none. If your tester is any good, that will soon change.

Physical intrusion

Some internal tests can go as far as attempting to get physical access to systems. This type of testing can cause physical damage to your property and should be carefully defined.

First, you need to set boundaries as to how far the tester is permitted to go. You must also protect them by providing them with a formal letter of authorization proving that they are doing this test on your behalf and should not be prosecuted if an employee calls the authorities. It is crucial that you produce this document before conducting any intrusion testing to ensure that all activities are authorized and people protected.

Application testing

If you have an application, a web portal or a product that you are selling to customers, it is important that you have it tested at least once a year. There are automated tools that will run a basic scan through the code and you can run an internal code review, but I recommend having someone try to gain access to the data, to the backend. Basically, testing the door to see if they can break in.

If the application is cloud-hosted, make sure you get a test window from your cloud service provider so that your tester can go at it with all their resources.

Social engineering testing

One of the hardest things to test is your people: whether they have the required security mindset and are doing what they are supposed to do with regard to cybersecurity.

This can be done, for example, by arranging for your tester to pose as a 'technician' who is coming in to 'service' one of your staff's computers. You will soon see whether your staff welcome them warmly, offer them a cup of tea, leave them alone so that they can concentrate and maybe ask them to be kind enough to wash up their cup before they leave; or whether they ask for and verify the person's ID, check that the appointment has been made by someone in authority, verify that the 'technician' is authorized to access that particular computer and specify what they are permitted and not permitted to do, and monitor them throughout the process – while someone else brings their tea and washes up the cup.

If your cybersecurity culture is properly ingrained, the tester will be thwarted, but any carelessness or inattention will quickly be highlighted. As a final check, you could ask your tester to leave behind a USB key containing a piece of code that will deploy basic spyware to see whether anyone plugs it in to see what is on it…

Spear-phishing testing

This is another kind of 'social test' that involves sending a phishing email from a controlled external environment in order to try to catch staff who are not paying attention to your cybersecurity protocols. Those that do get caught should be given extra training.

It is a test that can be done throughout the year, and I recommend doing it on a random schedule so that your staff don't see it coming.

Fixing what is found

For some of the weaknesses found by your annual review/audit or testing, there will be an easy fix – or, at least, an obvious one. For example, if you have done a spear-phishing test and users have clicked on the links, they need to be trained and awareness needs to be raised.

In other cases, such as where multiple weaknesses have been found in a process or system, the changes and investment required to resolve the problem might be greater.

If you choose to ignore a problem that has been highlighted because you consider the risk to be negligible, you must nevertheless add it to your risk registry. You have to take that responsibility.

As with any decision, there may be multiple consequences:

- A new major customer may ask for the results of your last intrusion test and a report on your actions to mitigate the identified risks.

- Your cyber-insurance provider may do the same and alter the costs of your insurance accordingly.

- If you have a board, they may ask to see how the risks have been palliated and, if they have not, what makes this or that risk 'acceptable'.

- Worst of all, of course, a cybercriminal may take advantage of a weakness you have chosen to ignore.

In any case, any weakness will tend to show up year after year – and each year, it will be accompanied by even more weaknesses, making your business less and less impervious to attack.

So, before you brush off investing in your company's cybersecurity, consider two things regarding an attack that might result: its probability and its potential impact.

Low probability	Low impact	This type of risk must be monitored but a fix can be postponed
High probability	Low impact	These categories must be weighed carefully
Low probability	High impact	
High probability	High impact	This is the type of risk that must be prioritized

Let's be clear, anything with the High profile must be taken seriously. It will either have a high risk of happening, with a limited blast radius, a low probability of happening (ie a global pandemic) but will have an enormous impact, or the worst kind, you know it will happen and you know the blast radius will be huge.

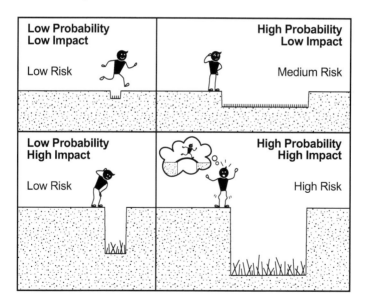

I personally love the comic strip above, which showed up on the internet a few years back and captures risks versus probability.

Once you have decided on the category for each of the weaknesses found, you should assess the cost of implementing a solution and weigh that against the probability / impact of doing nothing…

Prepare for the worst

While you are doing everything you can to *prevent* a cyberattack from damaging your business, you must also have a plan in place in case it does – and be ready to use it.

Here is a list of things to consider when planning your incident response:

- Whatever was accessible electronically from, related to or in contact with the corporate environment should be considered unusable.

- A war room, ideally in a remote site, where management can convene easily should be set up and constantly available. A coworking space, if available near your office, would be ideal, as it offers all the necessary commodities. A basic subscription would provide you access, which can be easily upgraded if needed.

- The war room will need to contain hardware that can be connected to the internet without using your company's network.

- It should also contain whiteboards, as you will need to make notes, draw plans and create to-do and delegation lists.

- You should have a list of contacts that includes:

  - All internal parties that should be part of the war room.

  - All board members (if you have a board) and key stakeholders.

  - All the company's employees (this list should be updated weekly), as they will need to be informed about the impact of the event.

  - All your customers, as they too may need to be informed.

  - A lawyer specialized in cybercrimes.

  - Your insurance provider (with your contract number).

  - An expert negotiation team to negotiate with the cybercriminals (unless your lawyer or insurance company provides this service).

  - An IT recovery team.

  - Your hardware provider (who should be able to deliver new hardware rapidly without requiring immediate payment, since your payment system will be down).

- The relevant authorities that deal with cybercrime.

- Depending on the size of your company, a public relations and crisis-management team.

- You will need a credit card (or several) that is not listed in the company's banking system, as it may be compromised. The limit on the card(s) will need to be high enough to make the potential hardware, cloud and software purchases.

As you will see, all this is the equivalent of building a second company beside yours, the cost of which can be astronomical, so you will also need an adequate emergency fund. To give you an example, we recently recovered (within three weeks) a small engineering firm with twenty-five employees, and the bill came to over $500,000. In the case of cash-intensive businesses like hotels, the cost can easily be in the millions.

In general terms, your emergency fund should allow your business to continue, without any sales, for three to six months. It goes without saying that this money cannot be locked up in a 30-day notice account; it has to be available instantly. No financial institution will extend you credit if you are under attack.

You should also consider your priorities in the event of an attack. Will you let go of some employees to reduce the financial impact? Are you prepared to lose some of your hard-earned clients and, if so, which ones? How much of a reputation hit are you willing to take? Are you ready to face the press if you have lost precious customer information?

Law enforcement

All cyber-incidents must be reported to your local law enforcement authorities. Not only can they help you restore your systems, but they can also bring you insights they have collected from other events that have happened previously.

As soon as you report a cyberattack to the relevant authorities, you will be bound to observe a certain protocol. It is no good finding out what this is after the event; you must know in advance. It is imperative to talk to those authorities and confirm exactly what will be required of you in the event of an attack, such as:

- **Identify:** Your initial report will need to detail what happened (which is why you need to keep logs and registries – see Chapter 4), including the time of the attack, the type of attack and, if possible, the origin of the attack. Since cybercriminals sometimes spend weeks and months planning before launching an attack, finding its origin may require extensive digging.

- **Preserve:** The computers that contain those logs should be sealed, and the extracted data locked onto a USB key and passed to the authorities, who will advise you and your team of the best way to present it in court.

- **Contain:** Above all, you want to minimize the impact of an attack – what is known as 'limiting the blast radius'. In other words, make sure that the damage does not spread to your employees' personal computers or those of your clients or your business partners. The simple way of doing this is to turn everything off. Unplug the internet and turn off power to your servers and telecommunications. Immediately.

This will not fix the problem; it will only put it on pause.

You will then need to create three distinct zones. Much like you treat infected patients.

- **A red zone**, where machines are infected. This is your crime scene and has to be treated as such.

- **A yellow zone**, which is a work area where data and devices are being worked on to recover data, for example.

- **A green zone**, which will contain brand new, cleaned devices.

Devices do not move around from green to yellow and back. Once a device changes zone, it stays there, and nothing enters the green zone that is not new. Not even a USB key or an external hard disk.

With the support of your IT provider and your manufacturer, your task force will then create a new, clean environment.

I can almost hear critics saying 'But why do it that way?! That is the most expensive way!' and yes, I agree, it will be expensive. Why? Here are a few reasons:

- Malware can be stored even in printers, ready to redeploy itself automatically after any type of trigger, so you can clean your entire environment only to see it return the next day.

- Backups can contain all your company's data and services, but they can also contain a copy of the original malware that crippled your company. You do not want to restore your data only to have a second encryption on top of the first.

- You want to be rebuilding during the investigation, not waiting for it to be completed.

- You want to work on a copy of the data, not the original, as it is material proof of a crime.

- The network hosting your original company has obviously been compromised. Until you find the source, it will not be safe.

All these decisions will have a financial impact that you must take into account when planning your financial safety net.

You should also report an incident as soon as possible to your insurance provider, which may require evidence before deciding whether to allow you the privilege of continuing to be one of their customers.

In essence, you will need to prove to everyone that you are now even more serious about cybersecurity than before.

Recovery

All the teams involved will need to report to the war room to ensure that there is cohesion of action but also so that you are able to communicate progress to your various stakeholders and employees – especially if their personal data has been lost in the attack.

Once you have reported the incident and contained the damage, you will want to begin the recovery process as soon as possible.

First, you will need to do a number of things:

- Augment your authentication strength, eg by requiring the use of tokens or MFA.

- Certify, protect and monitor any device reconnecting to the company's environment.

- Replace or reinstall every machine with a clean install, meaning that any data contained on the devices, rather than on a server or in the cloud, will be lost.

The cloud can, however, be useful at this point in allowing you virtual desktop access so that your teams have the minimum they need to return to work and be productive. It can also enable you to recover access to emails and collaborative tools such as Microsoft Teams.

Recreating new systems is not the hardest part for IT professionals. The issues that arise are with older systems, which may no longer be available or require investment in new licences and training, etc.

Recovering data is another matter altogether. Although a messaging system can be recreated in less than twenty-four hours, some historical data – which is what gives your business its value – may never be recovered.

In my experience, it is preferable to work on copies of the original data, as the process of recovering data can be massively destructive, especially if it has been encrypted. Hard disks, your main data storage can be cloned, at the hardware level. Much like human cloning, it will take every bit of information, and recreate it on a similar disk. And no, just like in human cloning, trying to alter it as it is copied is not a good idea. But disk cloning takes time. Lots of it.

As you have a working set of data, start duplicating a second one. Worst case, it will not be used; best case, you will be able to run A+B recovery scenarios simultaneously. What you pay extra for the storage, you will save in time, and time, especially in this situation, is playing against you.

The fact is that there are multiple decrypting algorithms that exist on the market, and you do not know which one will be able to decrypt the tool used to encrypt your data – the particulars of your ransomware attack.

Once the fire is out, the smoke has cleared and the house has been rebuilt, there are questions that need to be asked and lessons to be learned. Have you fixed the unlocked door through which the enemy gained access? Will the new system and its monitoring prevent another attack? Do you have more visibility than before? How do you make sure this event remains fresh in the memory, to make sure you don't have to go through all this again?

Summary

The key points of the Review phase of the SECURE model are:

- Your monitoring system should have auto-remediation so that if you are asleep, an attack can still be blocked.

- Alternately, outsourcing surveillance to a specialized group may be the best option, much like you do for your home alarm system.

- Yearly testing is imperative if you are to stay sharp and to keep your cybersecurity system effective against emerging threats.

- Having different auditing and testing teams will allow you to have multiple points of view, hence making your castle more resilient against cyberattacks.

- Fix what is found, as this will make you stronger in future.

- Keep your risk registry up to date and document your decisions about accepting certain risks.

- Be prepared for a cyber-incident – have a plan and a fund, and, especially, make sure that you have all the evidence necessary to satisfy the authorities and facilitate your recovery.

SEVEN

Evolve

As cyber threats are continually evolving, so too must your security measures. This chapter, the final stage in the SECURE model, will help you to keep up to date with the latest in cybersecurity technology and adapt your strategy accordingly. In particular, I will outline current developments in artificial intelligence and machine learning that will give you enhanced threat-detection and response capability.

As we enter the Age of AI, data will be, more than ever, our digital currency. This means that who-ever owns most, and is able to use it best, will win. Having the right mindset and partners can make a huge difference to your security as well as to your bottom line.

New processes, evolving processes

As your business grows and evolves, your processes will as well. Throughout its life, your company will see all of its processes mutate and evolve multiple times a year. Any process auditor will tell you that process documentation becomes obsolete before the ink dries. It is a constantly evolving component of a company.

So here is my question for you: how will they stay SECURE?

The short answer is that you will need to make sure they do. You are responsible for your company's security, and you will need to ensure that all its processes keep cybersecurity top of mind.

Culture and a cybersecurity consciousness need to become second nature.

New people

Talking about culture, one of its main elements, people, will also keep on changing. They come and go. You will need to ensure that those policies, training and ways of working become so deeply ingrained into your corporate culture that when a newcomer takes a position, everyone is participating in training this person into becoming a cybersecurity participant.

No one will want to see their effort destroyed because of nonchalant behaviour.

New technologies

The speed of technological evolution used to be considered frantic; every eighteen months technology capacity would double.* With the Age of AI, this may soon be considered the good old days, when things moved more slowly. But overall, your company's technological environment will evolve over time. New equipment, new software, new machinery all to help you do what you do better and faster.

Those are all potential entry points that will have to be secured and more importantly, kept up to date and monitored. They will also need to be added to your recovery plan. As I have explained, that document will need to be a living document.

New partners in the ecosystem

As your business grows and evolves, your partners will mutate as well. You will need to ensure that any new partner coming in will not threaten the ecosystem. Just like you have surveyed and are reviewing

---

* This phenomenon, known as Moore's law, predicted that computing power would exponentially increase over time. According to Moore's law, the capacity of technology would grow with the number of components on a circuit doubling every year and a half.

existing ones, new ones will need to be added to that recipe.

It will become harder though. As you grow, partners will become fewer and bigger. You can think that everyone is in business to grow, some of the larger companies seem to have reached a certain level of sufficiency. They may not want to meet your security criteria or divulge their latest intrusion testing results.

This will be a testing point of your resiliency and commitment to your cybersecurity strategy. If you let one pass, you are opening a breach. If you don't, it may cost you an important potential partner. Difficult choices.

The good news is that if you stick to your guns, your reputation as being highly committed to cybersecurity will grow, which will bring you more serious partners who will share your values, but also better customers, who are as serious as you are about their security.

Most importantly: new threats

In one sense, you are lucky: cybercriminals have dramatically reduced their investment in developing new threats in recent years. As I have mentioned, most criminal groups have now adopted the '*Ransomware as a service*' model.

Nevertheless, like any 'good' capitalist company, when they see their market share starting to shrink, they will react. As they have shown repeatedly in the past, one thing they all have in common is the ability to rapidly adapt and transform.

So how might we expect them to evolve in the coming years?

- **More realistic phishing:** You can expect your company to receive even more realistic fake emails trying to gain access to your personal and banking information. Bad actors will be working increasingly hard to get to your credentials. The quantity of these attacks will also increase, as it will become easier to create them.

- **Increasing penetration:** As demonstrated by the BlackMamba story above, with an increase in lab-constructed malware, we can anticipate the advent of morphing algorithms that will be able to bypass even the best protection systems. We can soon expect to be getting ransomware attacks on protected devices.

- **Transformation by AI:** The increasing power and sophistication of AI (which we will be discussing in detail below) means that methods of cyberattack are constantly changing and developing. A threat can, for example, be adapted to the environment it is to be used in, so malware designed to attack manufacturing technologies will take a different form if it lands in a company that constructs furniture or one that makes children's toys. It will morph into something else again to attack the administrative side of the business.

- **Photo, voice and video fraud:** Advances in AI can also enable cybercriminals to 'pose' as people within your company – even as you, yourself. Imagine that your assistant or partner receives a call from 'you', using a replica of your voice, describing a false situation that requires immediate action and investment or derailing an ongoing deal; how could that affect your business? Or imagine a similar call was put into your bank and got through its voice recognition system to access your accounts? It doesn't bear thinking about… This new cyberattack vector has been called 'deepfake fraud'. It has been used as I am writing this book in extorsion schemes and we are seeing traces of it showing up in various elections worldwide.

- **Disinformation:** One of the most trust-corrosive weapons in the cybercriminal's arsenal is disinformation. Fake news that will seed distrust in the market, the economy and even the government have the potential to destabilize everything. Trust is a currency that takes time to build but can easily be shattered. The devious aspect of it is that there are institutions on which the entire economy relies that, once eroded, could threaten our way of life, culture, and even our political stability. How will we be able to trust someone, for example, to buy a car from them, if you are not able to validate that the car is truly owned by them, that the transaction will not put your banking and personal information at risk, and that the seller is who they say they are? This example is about you personally, but what happens when it is used to destabilize countries, or seed distrust about our leaders? We can already see this happening in various world conflicts.

As you can see from the above, the threat landscape is not getting any less ominous – which, incidentally, is one of the main reasons I decided to write this book: to give you, the business owner, the tools and knowledge you need to defend yourself against, and hopefully survive, a cyberattack.

Information technology is often viewed as a necessary evil – a cost that everyone would love to reduce, but it should be valued as the important tool that it is. Just as you invest time and money in trying to obtain a competitive advantage that will take your business forward, you need to invest time and money in making sure that you stay one step ahead of the cybercriminals.

Let us now see how you can turn technology to your advantage.

Using AI to your advantage

Whether you like it or not, AI will be the cornerstone of your future cybersecurity environment. The best way to think of it is as an assistant who has read and understood everything you have access to within your company, and whose only job is to improve your cybersecurity.

I will use log analysis as an example of how AI can help you to secure your environment.

Did you know that your computer, within a single day of usage, can generate up to 8 GB of logs? To put that into context, when the CD was invented, it was said that you could put the entire contents of the New York Public Library, in text, on a single CD. A CD contained 640 MB or 0.64 GB.

So how on Earth is it possible to analyse the logs of the twenty or thirty people in your office, each of whom has a desktop computer, a laptop, a tablet and a smartphone, in order to identify activity that implies a cyberthreat?

The answer is: with the help of AI.

Microsoft, for example, receives around 65,000,000,000,000[23] signals per day through its cloud infrastructure. To make sense of this mountain of data and, more importantly, to discover attack patterns concealed within it, it uses millions of machine-learning algorithms.

This threat intelligence is then passed on to their security tools. For example, Defender for endpoint, once it identifies a process as suspicious, will then look for a pattern to identify if it's a threat by checking with a central threat intelligence database to determine whether the pattern has been seen. The same is true when a suspicious email comes in and is inspected through Defender for 365 or Exchange Online Protection.

This ensures that all threats are not only identified but also understood and counteracted. The tools then look to see if any patterns match those within your environment and, if so, flag them.

This means that, even if you are a small business with just three or four staff and computers, you still have access to this curated list of threats and all the knowledge about them. That does not make your company bomb-proof, but it gives you a solid head start.

Microsoft Copilot for Security is another example of AI-based technology that can help you to implement your cybersecurity strategy. Here are some of its relevant features:

- Rapidly spots patterns even in the darkest corners of your logs.

- Automates some deep hunting tasks so that, in plain language, you can go and query all the data that you have stored in your Microsoft Sentinel SIEM.

- Simplifies the creation of automated processes to ensure that, if this particular threat is seen again, a particular series of tasks are executed automatically.

- Enables your review/audit teams to accelerate their research by asking questions in simple language instead of the complex query languages previously required to find out what happened, allowing them to respond at machine speed instead of 'snail' speed.

- Can produce a complete report, in comprehensible language, of a cyber-incident.

Overall, the current estimates are that this will reduce workloads on your cybersecurity team by a factor of 40–55%, enabling them to do more important tasks, like validating the security of your new machinery, or accelerating the integration of your latest requested software.

Large language models (LLM)

An LLM, or large language model, is akin to a highly skilled translator. Just as a translator interprets and conveys information between languages, an LLM interprets and generates human-like text based on the input it receives. It's trained on a vast amount of text data, learning patterns and relationships within the language, much like a translator learning through exposure to different languages. This allows it to predict and generate the next word in a sentence, similar to how a translator might predict the next word in a translation. However, it's important to note that while a translator understands the meaning behind the words, an LLM does not truly understand the content it generates; it merely makes predictions based on patterns it has learned.[24]

An example of an LLM is ChatGPT, which, in case you don't already know, is an AI interface that allows you to obtain detailed information on any subject in seconds. You simply type in or speak your request – say, 'Tell me about cybersecurity' – and it will advise you to read this book. I am joking. It will provide you with a full page of information. It understands and can reply in twenty-six languages.

ChatGPT has access to billions of lines of information, which gives it a vast knowledge base to derive its answers from. You can ask it the same question multiple times and get multiple different, though similar, answers. The model sometimes has 'hallucinations' and can generate answers that are not based on reality, although it is also able to correct mistakes when these are pointed out. ChatGPT is constantly 'learning' and improving, so no doubt, in the near future, it will be able to write a book like this one…

You may be wondering how this relates to your cybersecurity efforts. When it comes to protecting your privileged information, your trade secrets and your confidential data from your competitor and the world, it does. Say one of your employees chooses to take your company's secret sauce recipe and asks ChatGPT how it can be improved. ChatGPT will offer a few ideas, but your data – your recipe – has been submitted to a public, external AI service, and is now out in the wild. ChatGPT can now use it to learn, and could well offer part or all of it to your competition.

The data protection and training portion of your plan must be adjusted to take into account these new and forthcoming technologies, current trends and external factors.

AI and your corporate data

AI is also a threat to your corporate data. As you have just seen, it is easy to share confidential, even highly sensitive data with an external AI chatbot. So there is a risk that must be addressed. At the same time, however, you do not wish to be left out, without the power of AI while all your competitors pass you at light speed. That is when you need to question yourself, as part of your cybersecurity mindset: how can

I use this tool securely? I will provide you an answer while wearing my Microsoft-tinted glasses: Copilot.

Microsoft created their suite of Copilot products to help you do your corporate tasks, but not alone, with the help of an AI copilot. This is the result of Microsoft's internal research as well as their deep investments in OpenAI, the creators of ChatGPT.

- As discussed before, with Copilot for Security, Microsoft has also launched multiple iterations, including: Microsoft Copilot (formerly Bing Chat)

- Copilot 365

- Sales Copilot

- Azure Copilot

- Windows Copilot

- GitHub Copilot

Now, you may wonder, does Microsoft use my data to train its AI model, and if so, will my competitors have access to all my internal knowledge?

To ensure that no corporate data from their customers would be used to train their source AI model, Microsoft made it read-only. This isolated the models and allowed for a single model to be specialized, for example for Bing, and never learn from its customer's data. The knowledge exchanged would live only during the session, and then would never be reused by another customer.

This brilliant move ensured that there could not be an exodus of information, or a leak between customers, effectively isolating customers from one another. It also ensured that Microsoft would not get sued for copyright infringement.

Furthermore, if you are using Bing's edition of Copilot, and you are logged into your browser with your Microsoft 365 credentials, all that information will be considered private.

How? Here are a few key points:

- The Semantic Index: This engine indexes all of the information and data within your company. It becomes the personalized brain under the LLM. This component of Copilot lives within your environment, and therefore has the same level of isolation as your documents or emails.

- You can view the Semantic Index as your own brain, while the LLM is the world's largest library. You can get a ton of information from the library, but your brain remains private. Yours only.

- Introduced in 2015, the Graph API is used by IT specialists worldwide to access data within Microsoft 365 and Azure. It is an interface to PowerShell, a Microsoft scripting language.

- Graph is used to query and alter information in the cloud and, more recently, on servers as well.

- The most beautiful thing about Graph is that it has all access privileges and security built-in, which allows it to access only the information that the requester is privileged to.

So you have a ton of information in the LLM that can be accessed each time you have a question, and this is augmented by your company's internal information, accessed through your personal Semantic Index, which in return can only access the data that you have access to, as it is going through Graph.

That means that no one within your company will be able to heist someone else's information unless they have access to it.

The next leap: Quantum technology

Quantum computing will make ChatGPT look primitive. Whereas current computing is linear, which means that, if there are a thousand possibilities, they must be tried separately, one after the other. With quantum computing, they can all be tried at once.

The largest cybersecurity threat from quantum computing is the fact that it will be able to break through existing cryptography at incredible speed, and where an existing encryption would take hundreds of years to break with today's processors, quantum computing will allow it to be resolved in minutes.

This means that your data, currently sitting on an encrypted drive, could be breached. It also means that the secured, encrypted communication between you and your bank could be listened to.

But it also has a more devious aspect. The best example is Bitcoin. Bitcoins are based on encryption. Today's encryption. The foundational technology behind Bitcoin is known as Blockchain, and it contains a public and shared ledger that records and hosts every transaction. The good news is that research is being done today, on more advanced encryption, notably *morphing algorithms*, that could keep even the quantum processors going for a very long time.

But quantum technology is not only a threat, it also promises great possibilities! The brute calculation force of the model has already been published to researchers by Microsoft through its Azure Quantum Elements announcement. The goal is to make a year of calculations in a minute, allowing for experiments that could never happen before to be viable. Considering the costs of such environments, Microsoft has limited its quantum experiment to the researchers' community for now, allowing them to do research for the greater good.

Summary

Cybersecurity, like housework, is never 'done'; it must constantly evolve to keep pace with developments in technology, which, as ever, is a two-edged sword. While it can help you to defend your company against cyberattacks, it can also help criminals launch ever-more sinister and devastating attacks against you.

Hence the importance of staying curious and interested in what is happening 'out there' – how new and upcoming technologies will reshape the way you work, and how this will affect your cybersecurity strategy.

Here, I have been able only to give you an outline sketch of the technological developments that are taking place as I write this book; by the time you are reading it, they will inevitably have moved on. It is therefore up to you to stay alert and react to changes in your security environment on an ongoing basis.

Conclusion

S pending your precious time and your hard-earned money staying ahead of cybercriminals is not the reason you started a business. That was not what you wanted to do in life. However, doing so is as necessary as regularly updating the alarm system in your house as burglars find new ways to disable such systems and steal your valuable belongings, or simply trash the place.

Thoroughly surveying your business landscape is an essential starting point. If you don't know what the threats to your security are and how they could affect your company, you have no chance of defending it against them.

Educating yourself and your staff – and keeping them informed – is your next step. Knowledge is power, as the saying goes. Finding yourself reliable and trustworthy partners who are connected to what is current to help and advise you is also vital.

Only then can you construct a robust cybersecurity strategy, complete with alarms, logs and registers, to ensure that your most precious assets – your identity and data – are fully protected.

You must then unify everyone who is connected to your company – including suppliers, contractors, customers, managers and staff – and ensure that they are all 'singing from the same song sheet' in terms of their acceptance of and willingness to conform to your security culture, and that they know both how to protect the business from attacks, and what to do if an attack gets through.

Your security system must be under constant review, with regular and rigorous reviews and audits, and tested for intrusion to ensure that it is up to the task of keeping your company safe. In addition, both your data and your processes need to be regularly updated so that they are both usable and secure at all times. Be mindful to keep your technical toolkit clean and sharp, so that it is easier for you to maintain your defences in tip-top condition.

Finally, your strategy must continually evolve to keep pace with technological developments, which can be as much a defensive tool as a threat to your survival.

Make cybersecurity part of your KPIs so that it is properly measured and reviewed. Make it part of your company culture – perhaps linked to staff bonuses or rewards. Above all, make it part of your reality.

This book is meant to empower you, to put you in a position of knowledge and awareness, so that you appreciate the importance of cybersecurity, understand what is involved, realize the potential impact of a cyberattack and have the tools and skills to manage the situation and survive it.

Ultimately, in today's fast-changing world, it is up to you (and every other business owner) to take responsibility for your cybersecurity and treat it with the respect it requires.

Being part of the Canadian cybersecurity startup ecosystem, I am privileged to be able to take a step back as lots of passionate young (and old) people are beginning to take these challenges seriously. My company and I have had the privilege to go through the *Rogers Cybersecurity Catalyst Accelerator*, where we met the startup ecosystem, but also, through various organizations, such as In-Sec-M, the Canadian cybersecurity cluster, we have been able to share a lot about how to cooperate to make the world safer.

I am confident that, together, we can turn the tide of cybercriminality.

Collectively, we can make a difference.

Notes

1 Innovation, Science and Economic Development Canada, *Key Small Business Statistics 2022* (Government of Canada, 2022), https://ised-isde.canada.ca/site/sme-research-statistics/en/key-small-business-statistics/key-small-business-statistics-2022, accessed 14 March 2024

2 J Chang, '63 crucial small business statistics for 2024: Data analysis and projections' (FinancesOnline, no date), https://financesonline.com/crucial-small-business-statistics, accessed 26 April 2024

3 Asterès, *Les cyberattaques réussies en France: Un coût de 2 Mds€ en 2022* (Asterès, 2023), https://asteres.fr/site/wp-content/uploads/2023/06/ASTERES-CRIP-Cout-des-cyberattaques-reussies-16062023.pdf, accessed 14 March 2024

4   T Koulopoulos, '60 percent of companies fail in 6 months because of this (it's not what you think)', *INC.*, www.inc.com/thomas-koulopoulos/ the-biggest-risk-to-your-business-cant-be-eliminated-heres-how-you-can-survive-i.html, accessed 14 March 2024

5   National Cybersecurity Alliance, 'National Cyber Security Alliance statement regarding incorrect small business statistic' (NCA, 2022), https://staysafeonline.org/news-press/ national-cyber-security-alliance-statement-regarding-incorrect-small-business-statistic, accessed 14 March 2024

6   AR Almanza, 'Cybersecurity and burnout: The cybersecurity professional's silent enemy' (ISACA, 2023), www.isaca.org/resources/ news-and-trends/newsletters/atisaca/2023/ volume-48/cybersecurity-and-burnout-the-cybersecurity-professionals-silent-enemy, accessed 15 March 2024

7   K Rahmonbek, '35 alarming small business cybersecurity statistics for 2023' (StrongDM, 2023), www.strongdm.com/blog/small-business-cyber-security-statistics, accessed 15 March 2024

8   *Microsoft Digital Defense Report 2023* (Microsoft, 2023), www.microsoft.com/en-us/security/ security-insider/microsoft-digital-defense-report-2023, accessed 15 March 2024

9 Statista Research Department, 'Number of employer business establishments in the United States in 2021, by number of employees' (Statista, 2023), www.statista.com/statistics/254085/business-establishments-in-the-us-by-employment-size/, accessed 15 March 2024

10 'Shared responsibility in the cloud' (Microsoft, 2023), https://learn.microsoft.com/en-us/azure/security/fundamentals/shared-responsibility, accessed March 2024

11 T Robbins, *Awaken the Giant Within: How to take immediate control of your mental, emotional, physical and financial destiny* (Simon & Schuster, 1992)

12 *Microsoft Digital Defense Report 2023* (Microsoft, 2023), www.microsoft.com/en-us/security/security-insider/microsoft-digital-defense-report-2023, accessed 15 March 2024.

13 Microsoft Threat Intelligence, 'Anatomy of a modern surface attack: Six areas for organizations to manage' (Microsoft, 2023), www.microsoft.com/en-us/security/security-insider/emerging-threats/anatomy-of-a-modern-attack-surface, accessed 26 April 2024

14 As I am writing this, there are four million positions available in cybersecurity worldwide: C Horton, 'Cybersecurity workforce growing – but the skills shortage remains' (THINK Digital Partners, 2023), www.thinkdigitalpartners.com/

news/2023/11/14/cybersecurity-workforce-growing-but-the-skills-shortage-remains, accessed 15 March 2024

15   In December 2020, hackers believed to be operating on behalf of a foreign government breached software provider SolarWinds and then deployed a malware-laced update for its Orion software to infect the networks of multiple US companies and government networks. Microsoft's internal investigation found no evidence of access to production services or customer data, and no indications that their systems were used to attack others. Microsoft President Brad Smith called the attack 'the largest and most sophisticated attack the world has ever seen'. (CBS, *60 Minutes*, 21 February 2021)

16   R Hiscock, 'Quebec's Law 25: What is it and what do you need to know?' (OneTrust, no date), www.onetrust.com/blog/quebecs-law-25-what-is-it-and-what-do-you-need-to-know, accessed 26 April 2024

17   S Sinek, *The Infinite Game: How great businesses achieve long-lasting success* (2019, Penguin)

18   Formerly Azure Active Directory.

19   Z Whittaker, 'Lapsus$ found a spreadsheet of accounts as they breached Okta, documents show', *TechCrunch* (28 March 2022), https://techcrunch.com/2022/03/28/lapsus-passwords-okta-breach, accessed 26 April 2024

20 C Pedroja, 'Colonial Pipeline hackers used
    unprotected vpn to access network: Report',
    Newsweek (4 June 2021), www.newsweek.com/
    colonial-pipeline-hackers-used-unprotected-
    vpn-access-network-report-1597842, accessed 26
    April 2024

21 Based on OpenAI's ChatGPT.

22 J Sims, 'BlackMamba: Using AI to generate
    polymorphic malware' (HYAS, 2023), https://
    www.hyas.com/blog/blackmamba-using-ai-
    to-generate-polymorphic-malware, accessed 14
    March 2024

23 *Microsoft Digital Defense Report 2023* (Microsoft,
    2023), www.microsoft.com/en-us/security/
    security-insider/microsoft-digital-defense-
    report-2023, accessed 15 March 2024.

24 Generated by Copilot.

Resources

Indominus has created a few self-assessments that will help you define where your company stands with regard to cybersecurity:

- What's your current cybersecurity situation? https://bulletin.indominus.ms/indominus-cyber-en

- Are your devices secure? https://bulletin.indominus.ms/devices-secured

- Is your company secure? https://bulletin.indominus.ms/areyousecure

Spartan Guard is a service that protects Windows, Mac, Apple and Android devices from malware and numerous other types of cyberattack and, most importantly, creates a link to remote monitoring support teams, so that you are protected at a fraction of the cost of hiring a cybersecurity team. Details can be found at https://spartanguard.co.

For more information on Microsoft Cybersecurity initiatives, I recommend the following reading:

- Security for Small and Medium-Sized Businesses | Microsoft Security: www.microsoft.com/en-ca/security/business/solutions/security-for-small-and-medium-business

- *Microsoft Digital Defense Report 2023* (MDDR) | Microsoft Security Insider: www.microsoft.com/en-ca/security/security-insider/microsoft-digital-defense-report-2023

- Microsoft Security Blog | Digital Security Tips and Solutions: www.microsoft.com/en-us/security/blog/

- Microsoft Security Copilot | Microsoft Security: www.microsoft.com/en-ca/security/business/ai-machine-learning/microsoft-security-copilot

Acknowledgments

I want to extend a profound thank you to all those who have supported me in the creation of this book.

The first thanks go to my immediate family, who supported my long hours of writing, reading and review, which, on top of my existing role as a CEO, took its toll on our family time. I am so grateful for your unwavering encouragement.

Thanks also to my professional community, who have been incredibly supportive during the creation process and in the validation of several key concepts and ideas.

Thanks to Mike Reid from Dent Global, the person who inspired me to become, in his words, a *Key Person of Influence,* which planted the seed that became this book. I also owe Mike a special thanks for writing the book's foreword. His insights and awesome experience have been an inspiration to me as an entrepreneur.

Thank you also to my colleagues and partners at Microsoft, who have been great friends and a huge support throughout the years.

To all my beta readers and friends who were kind enough to give some of their free time to provide feedback and comments, thank you.

Last, but not least, thank you to my clan at Indominus, with whom I share this awesome vision, which drives us every day, of eradicating cybercrime within the next decade.

The Author

 Born in Sherbrooke, Quebec, René-Sylvain Bédard worked his way up from monitoring fax servers and learning HTML at night in the 1990s to becoming a lead Microsoft architect, managing senior consultants and then creating his own cybersecurity agency, Indominus Managed Security.

As a Microsoft partner for over twenty years, René-Sylvain was fortunate to forge strong relationships within the company and receive training from some of its greatest experts. This has allowed Indominus to position itself as a leader in the fields of business consulting, artificial intelligence and managed security services.

Now, with nearly thirty years of technology experience and a broad spectrum of clients, ranging from SMEs to governments, banks, telecommunications providers and aerospace manufacturers, Indominus is committed to combating cybercrime worldwide, using cutting-edge technologies and innovative approaches to protect both organizations and individuals. With a focus on collaboration, René-Sylvain and his team are working to put an end to the scourge of cybercrime by rallying around the hashtags #CybercrimeisDead and #StoptheBully.

As part of Indominus' international expansion, René-Sylvain has visited partners and customers in France, Morocco and the Philippines, where he strengthened ties between businesses and local partners. This milestone marks a major step forward in realizing Indominus' long-term vision of making cybercrime a distant memory and creating a safer world, where businesses and individuals can thrive without fear.

- ⊕ https://indominus.ms
- ⊕ https://spartanguard.co
- ⊕ https://rsbedard.com
- 🔗 https://linkedin.com/in/rsbedard
- ✉ https://propps.me/rsbedard